MW00488461

BY DONALD HONIG

NONFICTION

Baseball When the Grass Was Real
Baseball Between the Lines
The Man in the Dugout
The October Heroes
The Image of Their Greatness *(with Lawrence Ritter)*
The 100 Greatest Baseball Players of All Time *(with Lawrence Ritter)*
The Brooklyn Dodgers: An Illustrated Tribute
The New York Yankees: An Illustrated History
Baseball's 10 Greatest Teams
The Los Angeles Dodgers: The First Quarter Century
The National League: An Illustrated History
The American League: An Illustrated History
The Boston Red Sox: An Illustrated Tribute
Baseball America
The New York Mets: The First Quarter Century
The World Series: An Illustrated History
Baseball in the '50s
The All-Star Game: An Illustrated History
Mays, Mantle, Snider: A Celebration
The Greatest Pitchers of All Time
The Greatest First Basemen of All Time
Baseball in the '30s
The Donald Honig Reader
Baseball: The Illustrated History of America's Game
1959: The Year That Was
American League MVPs
National League Rookies of the Year
National League MVPs
American League Rookies of the Year
1961: The Year That Was
The Power Hitters
The Boston Red Sox: An Illustrated History
The Greatest Catchers of All Time
The St. Louis Cardinals: An Illustrated History
The Chicago Cubs: An Illustrated History
The Greatest Shortstops of All Time
The Philadelphia Phillies: An Illustrated History

FICTION

Sidewalk Caesar
Walk Like a Man
The Americans
Divide the Night
No Song to Sing
Judgment Night
The Love Thief
The Severith Style
Illusions
I Should Have Sold Petunias
The Last Great Season
Marching Home

THE CINCINNATI REDS

AN ILLUSTRATED HISTORY

DONALD HONIG

Simon & Schuster
New York London Toronto Sydney Tokyo Singapore

Simon & Schuster
Simon & Schuster Building
Rockefeller Center
1230 Avenue of the Americas
New York, NY 10020

Designed by Robert Bull Design
Manufactured in the United States of America

1 3 5 7 9 10 8 6 4 2

Library of Congress Cataloging-in-Publication Data
Honig, Donald.
The Cincinnati Reds; an illustrated history / Donald Honig.
p. cm.
Includes index.
1. Cincinnati Reds (Baseball team)—History. I. Title.
GV875.C65H66 1992
796.357′64′0977178—dc20 91-44749
CIP

ISBN 0-671-76108-0

For my daughter, Catherine

ACKNOWLEDGMENTS

I am deeply indebted to a number of people for their generous assistance in photo research and help in gathering the photographs reproduced in this book. Special thanks go to Michael P. Aronstein and Chuck Singer of TV Sports Mailbag; to Patricia Kelly and her colleagues at the National Baseball Hall of Fame and Museum at Cooperstown, New York, and to Jon Braude, information director of the Cincinnati Reds and crack photographer, for the photo of Cincinnati's 1990 All-Star–Game Players on page 242, the photo on the bottom of page 246, and the photo of Jose Rijo on page 247. Thanks also to photographers Gregory E. Rust for the photos on the top of page 246 and on the bottom of page 247; Nancy Hogue for the photos of Will McEnaney and Rawley Eastwick on page 209, the photo of Ken Griffey on page 210, and the photo of Tom Seaver on page 223; and W. F. Schildman for the photo of Pete Rose at bat on page 227.

A special note of thanks to Bill Deane, chief research assistant at the National Baseball Hall of Fame Library at Cooperstown and to head librarian Tom Heitz.

Also, for their advice and counsel, a word of thanks to the following: Stanley Honig, David Markson, Lawrence Ritter, Douglas Mulcahy, Mary E. Gallagher, Louis Kiefer, and Mike and Jim Brookman.

CONTENTS

♦ ♦

INTRODUCTION

They pride themselves on being the oldest professional baseball team in the world, having been originally formed in 1869 by a couple of one-time cricket-playing brothers named George and Harry Wright. From that day to this, the Cincinnati Reds, like most ball clubs, have etched a history of peaks and valleys, presenting many of the game's most memorable players and some of its most celebrated historical moments.

The great slugger Sam Crawford played for the Reds at the turn of the century, and later the team boasted stellar outfielder Edd Roush and Hall of Fame left-hander Eppa Rixey. In 1919 the Reds unwittingly participated in the most famous and notorious of all World Series. It was in Cincinnati in 1935 that night baseball came to the major leagues. In 1938, Cincinnati's Johnny Vander Meer gave baseball one of its landmark achievements, back-to-back no-hitters. Shortly after, a pair of pitching marvels, Bucky Walters and Paul Derringer, abetted by catcher Ernie Lombardi and first baseman Frank McCormick, and others, brought the club two straight pennants.

In the postwar years Cincinnati baseball was highlighted by pitcher Ewell Blackwell (who in 1947 came within a whisker of emulating Vander Meer's feat), slugging first baseman Ted Kluszewski, and an array of heavy hitters who set home run records in the 1950s.

In 1956 the Reds brought up the man who many feel is the foremost player in club history, Frank Robinson, who in 1961 led the Reds to another pennant.

Cincinnati baseball reached its peak in the 1970s. Under Sparky Anderson there were pennants in 1970 and 1972, followed by the onslaught of the "Big Red Machine," world champions in 1975–1976 and perhaps the preeminent team in National League history. This spectacular combine included catcher Johnny Bench, third baseman Pete Rose, second baseman Joe Morgan, outfielder George Foster, first baseman Tony Perez, and shortstop Dave Concepcion. It was in his second stint with the Reds, as player-manager in 1984, that Rose broke one of baseball's mountaintop records—Ty Cobb's lifetime hit total of 4,191.

In 1990, a new galaxy of stars under freshman manager Lou Piniella gave the fans of Cincinnati another pennant and one of the most exhilarating of world championships—a four-game sweep of the formidable Oakland Athletics. After 131 years baseball in Cincinnati was as fresh and as unpredictable as ever.

O•N•E

THE CRADLE OF PROFESSIONAL BASEBALL

THE charming myth of Cooperstown notwithstanding, there remains no verifiable origin or starting point for baseball, nor can reasonable people agree whether the first game played under "modern" rules took place in 1845 or 1846 or whether it took place in the Murray Hill section of New York City or in Hoboken, New Jersey. There is no argument, however, about when and where the first professional team was formed—in Cincinnati, Ohio, in 1869. It was a significant event in the history of American sports.

Having evolved from an English game called rounders, baseball's growth and development in America was astonishingly rapid. It came so early in the country's history that it is conceivable that Revolutionary War veterans could have witnessed some of the early games played in New York and New Jersey in the 1840s.

Baseball's first rules were formulated and set down by twenty-five-year-old Alexander Cartwright, a New York bank teller and enthusiastic amateur athlete. It was Cartwright who conceived the idea of 90 feet between bases, thereby establishing forever the perfect distance for a race between a running man and the throwing of a cleanly fielded ground ball. Cartwright (along with his friends on the Knickerbocker Base Ball Club) also laid out the configurations of the field as well as the number of players on each side—nine—and how to position them. The game would undergo much fine-tuning over the next half-century, but the basic contours were there from the beginning.

The charm and lure of baseball spread rapidly; within a dozen years it was being played as far south as New Orleans and as far west as California. The spread of baseball was facilitated by the Civil War. With long spells of time on their hands during the lulls between battles, the encamped soldiers began playing the game, even, on occasion, declaring informal truces to permit contests between Union and Confederate soldiers. One game, played at Hilton Head, South Carolina, between teams drawn from the 165th New York volunteer infantry, was said to have attracted more than 40,000 spectators. This demonstration of interest infected many of the onlookers like a benign virus, and when they returned home after the war to their farms and villages around the country these men brought baseball with them.

It was then still a game played by amateurs, young men who took to the quiet fields and pastures of mid-nineteenth-century America for the sheer joy of it, watched by handfuls of interested spectators sitting under the trees or lolling on the grass.

Amateurs or not, the game assumed a growing importance in the lives of its practitioners—like those in Cincinnati, for instance. In the summer of 1866, a group of gentlemen got together and founded the Cincinnati Baseball Club. The club was composed largely of attorneys, many of them Yale and Harvard men, who found the team sport physically exhilarating and socially enjoyable. The team gained permission to use the grounds of the Union Cricket Club, and baseball began drawing some of the cricketeers into its ranks.

As baseball's popularity rapidly grew, not

Harry Wright started out playing cricket.

only in Cincinnati but all around the country, the demand for skilled players increased. Baseball as a pleasant pastime for amateurs was quickly becoming history.

By 1868, the Cincinnati Baseball Club—their team was known as the Red Stockings, for their scarlet hosiery—had four salaried players on the squad. One of the four was Harry Wright, then thirty-three years old. The English-born Wright (he had been brought to America at the age of one year) made his living as a jeweler. He was also a skillful cricket player, with particular talents for organization and instruction. In August 1865 he came to Cincinnati from New York to accept the position of instructor at Cincinnati's Union Cricket Club.

It was not long before Harry fell under the spell of baseball, a game he had played in New York with Alexander Cartwright's old Knickerbocker club. Recognizing Harry's leadership skills, the Cincinnati Baseball Club in the winter of 1868 asked him to organize a team made up entirely of professional players. This was a bold step, for baseball had hitherto conducted itself under the façade of amateurism, despite the fact that more and more teams around the country were luring talented players to their cities with promises of payment. Cincinnati's Red Stockings took the field in 1869 as America's first openly proclaimed professional baseball team, a landmark event in the history of American athletics.

A prominent local attorney named Aaron B. Champion was elected president of the Red Stockings; the team was managed by Harry Wright. The first roster of the first professional baseball team, along with salaries, looked like this:

Player	Age	Position	Salary
Harry Wright	35	Center field	$1,200
Asa Brainard	25	Pitcher	$1,100
George Wright	22	Shortstop	$1,400
Douglas Allison	22	Catcher	$800

Player	Age	Position	Salary
Charles Gould	21	First base	$800
Charles Sweasy	21	Second base	$800
Fred Waterman	23	Third base	$1,000
Andrew Leonard	23	Left field	$800
Calvin McVey	20	Right field	$800
Richard Hurley	20	Substitute	$600

Shortstop George Wright, the highest salaried man on the team, was Harry's brother. George, who died at the age of ninety in 1937, was what a later baseball generation would call "a franchise player." Born in New York City in 1847, George Wright was by all accounts a splendid athlete. While still in his teens, he played with teams in New York, Philadelphia, and Washington. Although these various teams were ostensibly still amateur, it seems unlikely that George would have been so mobile if he had not been being paid to play. By the time his brother Harry formed the Red Stockings, George was generally recognized as the best player in the east, and when the club became avowedly professional, Harry recruited him.

Contemporary accounts refer to George playing a deeper shortstop than anyone else, meaning the Red Stockings star must have possessed a strong throwing arm. He also dazzled the customers with acrobatic catches of line drives (players did not wear gloves in those days, except for the catcher, whose protection consisted of little more than an ordinary cold-weather glove), and he introduced various defensive innovations such as covering the bag when the second baseman was busy elsewhere.

George Wright, the first "franchise player."

The team traveled extensively (when they were home they played in a small park situated where Lincoln Park is now, adjacent to Union Terminal), taking on all comers. Traveling by boat, railroad, and stagecoach, the Red Stockings played in Cleveland, Buffalo, Boston, Philadelphia, New York, Chicago, Milwaukee, Albany, St. Louis, Omaha, Louisville, and other cities and towns, going as far away from home as San Francisco. Their arrivals in a city stirred the sporting blood of the locals, much as Babe Ruth's Yankees would in later years. Local interest was further piqued by the fact that the Red Stockings proved to be unbeatable, with some of their victories taken by scores of 103–8, 80–5, and 94–7. By season's end their record was an unblemished 57–0, with George Wright batting—for what the statistic is

The Opening Day parade at professional baseball's first ballpark. The date was May 4, 1869, at Cincinnati, Ohio.

worth—.629. (George was so popular that, echoing Henry Clay's famous 1850 dictum, certain fans announced that they "would rather be Wright than be president.")

Kept abreast of their heroes' exploits by telegraph wire, the people of Cincinnati took great pride in the team and when the Red Stockings returned home in midseason they were given a parade replete with flags, banners, and a marching band.

The Red Stockings ran their winning streak to 130 in 1870 before finally being upended in Brooklyn by the Atlantics on June 14. The Atlantics' victory, however, was tainted. The game was tied going into the eleventh inning, when the Red Stockings scored twice. In the bottom of the eleventh, the Atlantics scored 3 runs, with the assistance of an overzealous spectator, who rushed out of the crowd (estimated at around 9,000) and jumped on the back of left fielder Cal McVey as Cal was in the act of running down a batted ball. This bit of zealotry—which was not covered by any of baseball's existing rules—led to 3 runs and the Cincinnati defeat. (It was also the first recorded act in the long catalog of zany behavior by Brooklyn fans.)

After the Red Stockings lost a few more games, Cincinnati fans, unused to defeat, began losing interest in the club. Waning local interest was only one of the reasons for the disintegration of the team. The success of the Red Stockings had stimulated interest in baseball around the country, leading to the formation of other openly professional teams, some of whom were making lucrative offers to certain Cincinnati players that the Cincinnati Baseball Club was unable to match. So, after two triumphantly successful years, America's first professional baseball team disbanded.

Buoyed by the interest created by the Red Stockings, eight teams got together in New York City in March 1871 and formed the National Association of Professional Baseball Players, the forerunner of organized baseball. Ironically, Cincinnati, whose team had been most responsible for whetting America's appetite for the burgeoning young game, was not represented in the new league.

T▾W▾O

INTO THE NATIONAL LEAGUE, AND OUT

For five shaky years the National Association of Professional Baseball Players embodied and demonstrated the virtues and qualities of the fledgling game, but at the same time it put on full display many of the game's less appetizing aspects. Although there clearly was an enthusiastic audience for baseball, it was just as clear that certain iniquities would have to be rooted out if the public's love for and faith in the game were not to be destroyed.

There was no central disciplinary force in the new league. Betting on games was rampant, with gamblers moving among the spectators and taking action. In this heady atmosphere, with large sums of money exchanging hands, it wasn't too difficult to find players of convenient ethics willing to accept bribes to throw games. Also, players sometimes appeared on the field in various states of intoxication. Loud bursts of profanity hurled among the fans—as well as between fans and players—offended many and generally kept women from attending games. In addition, payrolls were sometimes not met, players jumped from one team to another, and franchises dropped in and out of the league.

William Hulbert, founder of the National League.

With the organization of the National League in 1876, the National Association disappeared like a sand castle at water's edge. Behind the new league was William Hulbert, a Chicago businessman and owner of that city's franchise in the National Association.

Hulbert felt that irresponsibility and instability were draining public interest in a game that clearly had a bright future in the United States. Baseball, in Hulbert's eyes, was like a gifted but wayward child crying out for supervision and discipline.

On February 2, 1876, Hulbert and other interested parties met in a New York City hotel and formulated plans for a new structure of professional baseball teams—the National League—that would not permit gambling, alcoholism, rowdyism, umpire abuse, or Sunday games and that would insist that member franchises lived up to their obligations, such as playing every scheduled game, meeting payrolls, and not trying to entice away one another's players. (Hulbert, the league's strong man until his death in 1882 at the age of fifty, insisted on strict adherence to league rules: When the New York and Philadelphia clubs decided not to play out their schedules in 1876, they found themselves booted out of the league.)

Limiting franchises to cities with populations of at least 75,000, the National League initially had eight teams: Chicago, Cincinnati, St. Louis, and Louisville in the west, and New York, Boston, Hartford, and Philadelphia in the east. The schedule would consist of seventy games and at the conclusion of the season the winning team would be awarded a pennant (not to cost less than $100, according to league stipulations).

The Reds began their National League history playing in a park called the Avenue Grounds, which was located on Spring Grove Avenue near Arlington Street, where they remained until 1879. In 1880 they relocated to the Bank Street Grounds, at the corner of Bank Street and Western Avenue, which was closer to the center of the city. Like all early ballparks, the grandstands were of wooden construction, vulnerable to fire, and on occasion, collapse.

So as the nation celebrated its centennial year, the National League opened up shop and began laying footprints on American history. Cincinnati's thirteen-man roster included first baseman Charlie Gould (who was also manager) and second baseman Charlie Sweasy, who had been members of the famous Red Stockings of 1869–1870.

Cincinnati's National League debut was an auspicious one—a 2–1 victory over St. Louis, in front of a crowd of more than 2,000. When the Reds won again the next day, baseball fever began returning to the city. The elation, however, was premature, for at season's end the club was waterlogged in last place with a dismal 9–56 record. The two men who did the bulk of the pitching, Dory Dean and Cherokee Fisher, had records of 4–26 and 4–20, respectively. (Most of the clubs in the league employed only one or two pitchers, who worked from 45 feet away. The pitching distance was later increased to 50 feet and in 1893 to the current 60 feet, 6 inches, the extra 6 inches due to a mismeasurement that was never corrected.)

With New York and Philadelphia having been thrown out of the fraternity (they were readmitted in 1882), it was a 6-team league in 1877, with the Reds again last, this time with a 15–42 record. Outfielder Lipman Pike, major-league baseball's first Jewish player, started the season as manager, but was soon replaced by outfielder Bob Addy. Pike remained with the club as first baseman, and led the league with 4 home runs.

The most notable member of the 1877 squad (in the eyes of history) was pitcher William Arthur ("Candy") Cummings, at 5 feet, 9 inches and 120 pounds a rail of a man. Cummings had pitched for Hartford in 1876, running up a commendable 16–8 record. He joined the Reds in 1877 and went 5–14. Cummings left in midseason, at the age of twenty-eight, finished with big-league ball; nevertheless, today he has a place in the Hall of Fame, thanks to his claim (substantiated by some, refuted by others) of having been the first man to throw a curveball. The Reds had another historical footnote on the pitching staff that year in Bobby Mitchell, the first left-hander in National League history.

The 1878 Reds, managed by former Red Stockings hero Cal McVey, stirred some of the old hometown pride with a second-place finish, built on a 37–23 record, with newcomer Will White (30–21) doing most of the pitching. With his brother Jim (known as "Deacon" for his abstemious approach to tobacco and alcohol) behind the plate, the

Whites formed baseball's first brother battery. Will was also the first man to wear glasses on the field.

Cincinnati had in its outfield that year twenty-year-old Mike ("King") Kelly, who would play just two years for the Reds before going on to Chicago and Boston and becoming one of the game's first superstars. Wherever he deployed himself, the charming, handsome Kelly was a hit in his own personal "3-B" circuit: baseball, barrooms, and boudoirs. When Chicago sold him to Boston in 1886 for $10,000, the sum was considered so stupendous that newspapers had to print copies of the relevant documents to convince an incredulous public.

The club the Reds finished second to in 1878 was Boston, which won its second pennant in a row. These Boston teams were managed by Harry Wright and featured his brother George at second base and shortstop. George, the one-time blazing star of the old Red Stockings, was little better than a .250 hitter in his half-dozen years in the National League.

After finishing just 4 games out of first place in 1878, the Reds had brimming hopes as the following season opened. But these hopes were not fulfilled as the team came in fifth with a 43–37 record, with White winning them all while pitching a bulging 680 innings. Deacon White was the manager for most of the year, being replaced by McVey at the tail end of the schedule.

The 1880 edition of the Reds dropped through the league like dead weight and finished last with a 21–59 record. Managed by catcher John Clapp, the team batted just .224, second lowest in the league's brief history, while the sturdy Will White worked to an 18–42 record. This dismal season ended with the Reds being booted out of the league.

The National League's constitution forbade the sale of beer in its ballparks. Cincinnati, home to many fine breweries, had been ignoring this stricture, and the league had been content to look the other way. In 1879, the city of Worcester, Massachusetts, began a brief three-year tenure as a National League franchise. A Worcester newspaper, with apparently nothing better to do, began writing indignant stories about Cincinnati's flouting of the rules. The Reds were also renting their field to amateur teams for Sunday games, and this, too, offended the Worcester sensibilities.

Mike ("King") Kelly (1878–1879), an early favorite in Cincinnati baseball history.

Unable to further overlook the Reds' infractions, league officials summoned club president W. H. Kennett to a meeting in Buffalo on October 6, 1880. Kennett defended his policies, saying that the club needed the revenue gained from the beer concession and from the Sunday rentals. He further stated that the club would continue these practices in 1881, pointing out that what was done in Cincinnati was no business of Worcester's. What was done in Cincinnati, Kennett was told, was the larger business of the league, and when Kennett refused to accede to its demands he and his ball club were promptly thrown out of the National League.

Cincinnati was without baseball in 1881, but a year later a new major league was formed to compete with the National League, the 6-team American Association, with the Reds a charter member. The new club played its games at the park abandoned by its predecessor, the Bank Street Grounds. They remained there until 1884 when yet a third major league, the 12-team Union Association, was formed, with Cincinnati a member of this league as well. This new club took over the Bank Street Grounds lease, forcing the American Association club to hastily construct a new park located on the site of an old brickyard on Western Avenue at Findlay, where they remained after the Union Association and its Cincinnati team folded its tents after a single season.

Bid McPhee (1890–1899).

The Reds remained in the American Association until 1889. The club had some success in this league, winning the pennant in 1882.

On November 14, 1889, the Reds were readmitted to the National League, under the ownership of Aaron Stern. Cincinnati's membership in the oldest continuous major league has been unbroken from that time to this.

It was a tumultuous time in big-league history, for in 1890 yet another major league was formed—the Players' League, which was an outgrowth of players who were dissatisfied with their employers in the National League and American Association. The dissatisfaction arose from salary caps and the reserve clause, that onerous ball-and-chain clause in every player's contract that bound him forever to the club, termination coming solely at the discretion of the club.

Although America's love affair with baseball was well documented, the country was unable to support three major leagues, and after one season the Players' League collapsed, but not without creating a legacy: the financial bath that washed away the new league also took its toll on the American Association, and after the 1891 season this circuit also became leaves in the history book, leaving the field to the National League. Absorbing the best franchises and players from their failed rivals, the National League in 1892 reorganized itself into an unwieldy 12-team structure that stood until 1901.

T▾H▾R▾E▾E

THE 1890S

THE 12-team National League was dominated throughout the 1890s by strong teams in Boston and Baltimore; the best the Reds could manage were third-place finishes in 1896 and 1898. Under manager Tom Loftus, the club finished fourth in 1890 and seventh in 1891.

The 1890 club featured twenty-one-year-old right-hander Billy Rhines, who posted a 28–17 record (in those days of small pitching staffs, Rhines's win total ranked no better than fifth in the league).

At second base, the Reds had the man considered by many to have been the best at that position in the nineteenth century, John ("Bid") McPhee. In an era when ball players had reputations for rowdiness and heavy drinking, McPhee was known for his quiet dignity. He joined the Cincinnati club of the American Association in 1882 and then joined the Reds when they reentered the National League in 1890. He played his entire 18-year major-league career with Cincinnati, a remarkable record in an age of appearing and disappearing leagues, ephemeral franchises, player pirating, and broken contracts.

A .275 lifetime hitter, Bid McPhee was noted for his defensive play. In an age of shoddy fielding, he set records for fielding average, made even more noteworthy because until 1897 he disdained wearing a glove (fielder's gloves were in general use by the mid-1880s). Conceding that "hot-hit balls do sting a little at the opening of the season," Bid maintained that "after you get used to it, there is no trouble on that score." The second baseman led the league in fielding nine times.

Another member of the Reds in the early 1890s was third baseman Arlie Latham, whose nickname was "The Freshest Man on Earth," and it did not mean that Arlie was perpetually covered with spring dew but that he was rather a sassy fellow with an impish sense of humor. Arlie joined the Reds in 1890, when he was thirty years old, after a seven-year stint with the St. Louis club in the

Frank Foreman (1890–1891, 1895–1896), right-handed pitcher.

Charles Comiskey (1892–1894), one of baseball's "founding fathers."

American Association. A .269 lifetime hitter, Latham was a whippet on the bases, stealing 87 in 1891.

Arlie's winning personality gained him friendships with everyone from the hearty beer drinkers of Cincinnati all the way up to England's King George V, whom the whimsical third baseman met during a world tour that teams of the era frequently took. Later, when he took up residence in the British Isles for a time, Latham tried to teach the king how to throw. "King George had only a fair arm," Arlie later confided to friends.

After the 1890 season, Aaron Stern sold the Reds to Indianapolis clothing merchant John T. Brush. In 1892, Brush hired as manager Charles Comiskey, whose name has carried through baseball history with the resonance of a founding father. Like Clark Griffith and Connie Mack, Comiskey began as a player, became a manager, and finally a long-time club owner (in Charlie's case, the Chicago White Sox).

Comiskey made his name as a first baseman with the St. Louis club of the American Association, which he also managed to four straight first-place finishes from 1885 through 1888. When the association collapsed in 1891, Brush quickly snapped him up to play first base and to replace Loftus as skipper. Charlie's playing days were nearly over; he played the full season in 1892 (batting .227) and parts of the next two before hanging up his glove.

Under Comiskey, the Reds finished fifth in 1892. Tony Mullane led the pitchers with 21 victories, although in those strong-armed days thirteen other league pitchers won more. James ("Bug") Holliday, an outfielder, was the league home-run leader with 13.

The 1892 season was an eminently forgettable one for Cincinnati fans, except for an extraordinary exploit on the last day of the season, one that demonstrates the unpredictability of baseball as well as how casually the game operated at the time. A twenty-two-year-old Ohio farmboy named Charles ("Bumpus") Jones walked into the Reds clubhouse and introduced himself to Comiskey.

"I'm a pitcher," Bumpus said.

"All right," said Comiskey, who must have been feeling whimsical at the moment, "then we'll let you pitch."

They slipped Jones into a uniform and, omitting the detail of a contract, sent him out to the mound to pitch against Pittsburgh. The game may have meant nothing in the standings, but it provided baseball with a charming bit of folklore, for the unknown Bumpus Jones did nothing less than pitch a no-hitter,

With a piece of paper for a base, Harry Vaughan (1892–1899) poses where most baseball "action" shots of the time were taken—in a studio. Harry caught and played first base and the outfield for the Reds.

fanning 3, walking 4, and winning by a score of 7–1.

The beginning of a long and brilliant career? No. The story ends right about there. Bumpus pitched a few games for the Reds the following season, proved to be a drumhead for the rat-a-tat of opposing hitters and quickly departed from the big-league scene, leaving behind a 2–4 record and one shining, improbable moment.

After their fifth-place finish under Comiskey in 1892, the Reds came in sixth in 1893, which was still first-division in the 12-team league but hardly anything for the fans to get excited about.

The 1894 club, the last managed by Comiskey, took a spill into tenth place. Joining the Reds that year was outfielder William ("Dummy") Hoy, whose nickname derived from the fact that he was a deaf mute. Although the twentieth may not have been the most genteel of centuries, in its latter years at least, it would not have tolerated a man with Hoy's handicap being known publicly as "Dummy." Hoy, who at 5 feet, 4 inches was the last man on the field to know when it was raining, gave the Reds a .312 season in 1894, his seventh in the majors after service in the American Association, Players' League, and National League.

It is said that it was in deference to Hoy that umpires began giving hand signals for safe, out, and strike calls. This tough little man, who came to the major leagues in 1888, enjoyed a wonderfully long life, dying (in Cincinnati) on December 15, 1961, at the age of ninety-nine.

Comiskey left Cincinnati soon after the expiration of his contract in 1894. Charlie now had grander things on his mind. The Western League, soon to become the strongest of the minors, had recently been founded. Byron Bancroft Johnson (known to all as "Ban"), a sportswriter on the *Cincinnati Commercial-Gazette,* and a close friend of Comiskey's, was elected president of the circuit. With

Dummy Hoy (1894–1897, 1902).

Ban's support, Comiskey organized the St. Paul franchise in the Western League, and the two men began making the plans that would one day lead them to declare their operation a major league—the American League.

With Comiskey gone, the Reds needed a manager, and the man that club owner John Brush selected was an eminent name indeed: William ("Buck") Ewing. Many an old-timer, fan and player alike, went to their graves insisting that the greatest catcher of all time was Buck Ewing. Born in Hoaglands, Ohio, in 1859, Buck began his big-league career in 1880 with the Troy, New York, club. From 1883 through 1889, he played for the New York National League club, building a lustrous reputation as a .300-hitting catcher with a powerful throwing arm. In 1890, he joined many of his dissatisfied colleagues in the short-lived Players' League, playing with the New York entry, then rejoined the New York Nationals for 2 years, played 2 years for Cleveland, and in 1895 took over as manager of the Reds. Now thirty-four years old, Buck's concession to time was to give up catching and play first base. He played only one more year before removing himself from the active rolls. (Buck's early election to the Hall of Fame in 1939 attests to the high esteem in which he was held.)

It was Ewing who convinced Brush that a preseason conditioning program would help the team. (The idea of spring training had originated with Chicago manager Cap Anson, who in the previous decade had begun taking his players to Hot Springs, Arkansas, to boil out their winter's elbow bending.) Under Ewing, the Reds took their first spring training at Mobile, Alabama, in 1895.

Despite all the huffing and puffing, however, the trail of the 1895 Reds led to eighth place. The club had five .300 hitters in the lineup—outfielder Dusty Miller was tops at .335—but this was deceptive. Since the recession of the pitching mound to 60 feet, 6 inches in 1893, baseball had become a hitter's game. With the pitchers still finding the new adjustment difficult to make, batting averages had sported wings. In 1892, the last year of the 50-foot distance, the league had averaged .245; in 1893 the league mark was .280; in 1894 it was .309; and in 1895, .296. Cincinnati's team average of .298 in 1895 was just above the league norm.

Ewing's 1896 club was a spirited one,

Buck Ewing (1895–1897), Cincinnati manager from 1895 to 1899.

holding down first place in mid-July, but then slipping to third, where they finished, 12 games from the top. The winners were the Baltimore Orioles, a slashing band of base-path marauders that featured John McGraw, Wee Willie Keeler, Hughie Jennings, Joe Kelley, Wilbert Robinson, and others. This team, considered by many as baseball's best until the 1927 Yankees, drew 24,944 customers to the ballpark at Findlay and Western Avenues (now known as Redland Field) on Sunday, July 19 (yes, they were now playing America's game on the Sabbath), the largest crowd to see a game in Cincinnati up to that time. The Orioles ruined the day by winning.

Ewing brought his club home in fourth place in 1897, in a 12-team league a commendable achievement. The Reds were abetted that year by first baseman Jake Beckley, acquired on May 27 from the New York Giants.

Beckley had entered the National League in 1888, playing for Pittsburgh before moving on to New York. In ninety-seven games with the Reds in 1897, Jake whacked the ball for a .345 average and maintained his solid hitting throughout his years in Cincinnati, posting averages of .294, .333, .341, .307, .331, and .327 before being sold to St. Louis in 1904. Jake's defensive work, however, did not match his lusty hitting, with a scattershot

First baseman Jake Beckley (1897–1903). He batted over .300 in six of his seven Cincinnati seasons.

Cincinnati third baseman Charlie Irwin (1896–1901).

throwing arm his chief liability. One afternoon this led to a most bizarre play. Pittsburgh's Tommy Leach hit a roller to Jake, which the Cincinnati first baseman ran in on, scooped up, and fed to the pitcher covering. The throw, as was Jake's wont, was wild and bounced past the pitcher. Always the hustler, Jake raced after the ball and by the time he picked it up Leach was heading for third base and giving no apparent sign of stopping, reasoning that with Beckley's untrustworthy arm, trying to score was worth the gamble. Jake saw what was happening and evidently agreed with Leach's thinking, for instead of throwing the ball the Reds first baseman decided to make a footrace out of it. As the two men converged on the plate, Jake at the last moment made a flying leap and tagged Leach out, so vigorously that he caved in three of Tommy's ribs.

The Reds had a pair of twenty-game winners in 1897 in Ted Breitenstein (23–12) and Billy Rhines (21–15). A left-hander, Breitenstein had been acquired along with catcher Heinie Peitz from St. Louis where they had been known as "the Pretzel Battery" for their habit of getting together after a game and enjoying a few steins of beer and a bowl of pretzels. Peitz remained with the Reds until 1904, catching and playing the infield.

Another addition to the 1897 club was shortstop Tommy Corcoran, obtained in a

Left-hander Ted Breitenstein (1897–1900), one-half of Cincinnati's "Pretzel Battery."

trade with Brooklyn. A .257 lifetime hitter, Tommy was one of the top fielding shortstops of his day, and when he played alongside the veteran Bid McPhee, whose career was then winding down, Cincinnati fans were treated to some of the league's snappiest double plays. Tommy played for the Reds until 1906.

The 1898 Reds gave the hometown fans an exciting season, posting a 92–60 record and finishing third, 11½ games out, behind strong Baltimore and Boston clubs. Ewing's pitching had been beefed up with the acquisition from Pittsburgh of strong-armed right-hander Emerson ("Pink") Hawley. Hawley had a twin brother, so identical that their mother had had to pin different color ribbons on them in order to tell them apart, a blue for one boy and a pink for the future pitcher, who thus acquired his unusual nickname.

Tommy Corcoran (1897–1906), one of the top fielding shortstops of his time.

Catcher Heinie Peitz (1896–1904), the other half of "The Pretzel Battery."

Hawley was 27–11, his win total third best in the league, while Breitenstein was 21–14 (with the small staffs then in use, the twenty-victory season was far from unique: in 1898 seventeen pitchers joined what today is known as the pitcher's "charmed circle").

Early in the season, on April 22, Breitenstein no-hit Pittsburgh, 11–0, the Reds' first no-hitter since the unlikely effort delivered by

Bumpus Jones on the last day of the 1892 season.

The Reds fell to sixth place in 1899, Ewing's fifth and last season as manager. The club marked the century's end by introducing two sterling young talents: nineteen-year-old outfielder Sam Crawford and twenty-year-old left-hander Frank ("Noodles") Hahn. A native of a Nebraska town with the picturesque name of Wahoo (which gave him the nickname "Wahoo Sam"), Crawford was a muscular 6-footer with a strong left-handed power swing. It was the beginning of a 19-year big-league career for Sam, during which he would crack an all-time major-league record 312 triples. Those who saw Sam in his prime later said that if he had played in the lively ball era he might well have set records for home runs instead of triples. Breaking into thirty-one games for the Reds, the youngster batted .307.

Hahn launched his career with a fine 23–7 record, including a league-leading 145 strikeouts. The slender lefty was not destined for a long career—only 8 seasons—but it was going to be a winning one.

And as if taking his cue from the shades of the departing century, Bid McPhee announced his retirement. After eighteen years of playing big-league ball in just one city (the first eight with Cincinnati's American Association club), the forty-year-old second baseman was calling it a career. With a .279 batting average in 1899 and with his fielding as smooth as ever, Bid's retirement evoked cries of regret and pleas for reconsideration. But the pragmatic Mr. McPhee, who worked as an accountant in the off-season, said in reply, "I know what I'm doing. The fans are never going to have a chance to urge that I be benched, or traded, or asked to retire."

Departing with Bid was manager Buck Ewing, whose contract was not renewed. The great old catcher, who went on to manage the Giants for the first half of the 1900 season, had not done badly in Cincinnati, finishing in the first division in four of his five seasons, but had been unable to bring the taste of victory to a city that was yearning for it.

And so with the arrival of young stars like Crawford and Hahn and the departure of veterans like McPhee and Ewing, Cincinnati was following one of baseball's ordained rhythms—the coming of the new, the passing of the old.

F·O·U·R

NEW CENTURY, NEW LEAGUE

After operating as a 12-club league for eight years, the National League in 1900 dropped four franchises—Louisville, Cleveland, Baltimore, and Washington—and trimmed down to a more workable 8-team structure. The league now had an alignment that would prove to be remarkably stable: Cincinnati, Pittsburgh, St. Louis, and Chicago as its Western Division; Brooklyn, New York, Boston, and Philadelphia as its Eastern. This formation would remain intact for more than half a century.

The disbanding of four franchises left some good ball players on the market (Honus Wagner, for instance, moved from Louisville to Pittsburgh), and their addition to the various remaining teams made the league stronger and competition better. The Reds, however, benefited little, finishing seventh.

As his new manager, Brush hired former Philadelphia shortstop Bob Allen, who lasted just the one year. Jake Beckley gave the club one of his best years with a .341 average and rookie outfielder Jimmy Barrett batted .316. Crawford, in his first full season, was a .267 hitter. Playing third base for the Reds now was Harry Steinfeldt, who would be traded a few years later to the Cubs, for whom he would anchor the bag on the famous Tinker to Evers to Chance infield.

Rookie right-hander Ed Scott, who pitched one year for the Reds and only two years in the big leagues, was the top winner at 17–21, followed by Hahn, 16–19. Noodles, who had become quite a favorite among Reds fans, provided his partisans with the year's highlight, a July 12 no-hitter against the Phillies.

Third baseman Harry Steinfeldt (1898–1905), a .312 hitter in 1903.

Adding to the woes of the 1900 season was a fire that burned down most of the Redland Field grandstand; temporary seating was hurriedly provided to enable the team to finish out the season. Rebuilding was not completed until 1902 and when it was, Redland Field had some striking features, most notably ornate pillars and columns that resembled the architecture at Chicago's Columbian Ex-

Noodles Hahn (1899–1905), Cincinnati's ace left-hander at the turn of the century.

position a decade earlier. The somewhat overcooked structure was labeled "Palace of the Fans" by the local press.

Another disaster, even greater than a grandstand fire, struck the Reds in 1900. During the season, the New York Giants made a conditional purchase of $1,500 for a young pitcher who was mowing them down for the Norfolk club of the Virginia League. The young man came to New York, lost the three decisions he was involved in and did not impress the Giants, who returned him to Norfolk. After the season, the Reds drafted him from Norfolk. So the Reds owned Christy Mathewson. But not for long.

On December 15, 1900, John Brush traded Mathewson back to the Giants even-up for Amos Rusie. Rusie had been one of the great pitchers of the 1890s, firing a fastball that earned the Indiana native the nickname "the Hoosier Thunderbolt." It was Rusie's blazing speed, in fact, that more than any other factor induced the lords of baseball to move the mound back from 50 to 60 feet. But by now Rusie's thunderbolts were little more than popgun shots. At the age of twenty-nine, he was burned out; he had not, in fact, pitched for two years, sulking back home in Indiana as a holdout. Rusie pitched in just three games for the Reds in 1901, was 0–1, and then went home for good. Mathewson went on to become the king of all pitchers, winning 372 games for the Giants over the next sixteen years.

John Brush, the man who traded Christy Mathewson to the New York Giants and then bought the Giants.

Cincinnati's Redland Field, also known as "Palace of the Fans."

Amos Rusie, the one-time "Hoosier Thunderbolt," whom the Reds received in return for Mathewson. He pitched in three games for the Reds in 1901 and then retired.

Why was this horrendously one-sided deal made? Was it a question of poor judgment or dubious ethics? Many suspected the latter, for John Brush was soon to sell his interest in the Reds and buy the New York Giants. It was said that Brush was aware of Mathewson's great potential and wanted to make sure that Christy was safely tucked away in New York when Brush arrived.

Cincinnati fans, being a sentimental lot, let it be known that they missed their old favorite, McPhee, and so when it came to naming a manager for the 1901 season Brush gave the job to the recently retired second baseman. Bid did his best, but there wasn't much that could be done. The team capsized early in the season, sank to last place and there remained, gasping away to a 52–87 record (the league was on a 140-game schedule then; in 1904 it was extended to 154).

The team's ineptitude in 1901 made Hahn's record the more impressive. The young lefty worked to a 22–19 ledger, leading the league with 239 strikeouts. On May 22, Hahn fanned 16 Boston batters in a 4–3 win, setting a 1-game (nine innings) team strikeout record that has been tied but never bettered.

Beckley batted .300 and led the league with 39 doubles (tying Wagner), but the club's big hitter was Crawford. Wahoo Sam batted .330, drove in 104 runs, and led the league with 16 home runs, a lusty total for the time;

Sam Crawford (1899–1902), the fine slugger whom the Reds lost to the American League.

in fact, it remained the National League record until 1911. (All records, league, team, and individual, are dated from 1901, which is generally recognized as the start of baseball's modern era.) Sam's long-ball swatting also remained the Cincinnati club record for a remarkably long time: not until Harry Heilmann hit 19 home runs in 1930 was Sam's mark broken.

The American League, under Ban Johnson's presidency, had been formed in 1901 out of the Western League and by 1902 there was hot and bitter open warfare between the two major circuits. The National refused to recognize its competitor, mocking and belittling it as a "minor league." But the upstarts had big-league money to spend and were systematically raiding their opponents' rosters. National League stars who succumbed to the siren call of the flapping checkbook included Cy Young, Jimmy Collins, Nap Lajoie, and John McGraw among others.

The interleague squabbles were a lawyer's delight as clubs went to court: there were suits and countersuits, threats and insults, fist shaking and nose thumbing. With the National League holding stubbornly to a $2,400

Catcher Bill Bergen (1901–1903), major-league baseball's weakest hitter. His .227 average for the Reds in 1903 was the highest of his 11-year career, during which he averaged .170 for 947 games. He was sold to the Dodgers in 1904.

salary cap, the newcomers, offering salaries as high as $4,000 a year, were able to keep luring players. Most state courts were ruling against the reserve clause and thus the jumpers were allowed to remain with their new employers.

The warfare reached its peak of absurdity during the 1902 season when the wily John Brush, still running the Reds, was part of a group that bought the American League's Baltimore franchise and promptly released all of its star players, including Cy Seymour, Joe Kelley, Roger Bresnahan, Joe McGinnity, and McGraw. All of these worthies were then signed by National League clubs, leaving Baltimore to finish out the season with a skeleton crew. (Ban Johnson, however, had the last laugh in this one: after the 1902 season he transferred the franchise to New York, and thus the New York Yankees were born.)

The Reds benefited from the Baltimore fallout by signing Seymour and Kelley, a pair of good-hitting outfielders. Seymour batted .349 for his half-season in 1902, while Kelley rang up a .321 average.

In the midst of all this, McPhee decided that managing was more headache than reward, and on July 11 the old second baseman handed in his resignation. He was replaced on an interim basis by the club's business manager Frank Bancroft, who ran the club for seventeen days before handing the reins over to Kelley. One of the great players of the 1890s with Baltimore and Brooklyn, the thirty-year-old Kelley's best days were behind him, although as playing manager he contributed some steady hitting to the Reds over the next few years.

There were still more changes in store for the Reds in 1902, and these were at the top. On August 9, it was announced that John Brush had sold the club to a group that included Julius and Max Fleischmann, of the gin and yeast family; George Cox, a Cincinnati political boss who was best known as the epitome of municipal corruption, and August

Joe Kelley (1902–1906), Cincinnati's player-manager in the early years of the century.

Herrmann, who at the time was president of the city's waterworks commission. (Brush went on to take over the New York Giants, where young Christy Mathewson had been safely cached.) Cox and the Fleischmann brothers turned the running of the club over to Herrmann, which turned out to be a most happy decision.

Known to one and all as Garry, Herrmann, forty-three years old when he took over the presidency of the Reds, was to become one of baseball's most well-known and re-

Garry Herrmann.

spected executives. Portly and genial, he was given to checked clothes, diamond rings, good food, and lavish parties. To old-timers in Cincinnati, the name Garry Herrmann was immediately evocative of open-air beer gardens, trays of foaming steins carried high on the fingertips of singing waiters, and hearty good times that got better and better in the retelling.

Shrewd and exuberantly convivial, Herrmann was the perfect man to run a business that was also an entertainment. For seventeen years he also helped to run baseball: after the two major leagues agreed to a peace treaty in 1903, a National Commission was formed as baseball's governing body to resolve all disputes. The commission was made up of the two league presidents and Garry Herrmann, whose good judgment and sense of fairness in resolving interleague disputes were seldom questioned.

Amid all the turmoil attendant on their 1902 season, the Reds finished fourth, despite some good hitting by Crawford (.333), Beckley (.331), and Peitz (.315), in addition to the solid half-season averages logged by Seymour and Kelley. The club's .282 average was the league's second best. Hahn again topped the pitchers with a 22–12 record and a 1.76 earned run average, second in the league. Crawford's 23 triples led the league and established a team record that stands to this day.

The formal treaty of peaceful agreement between the two leagues was signed on January 10, 1903, at Cincinnati's St. Nicholas Hotel. Although it brought a harmonious working relationship to baseball, it proved costly to the Reds. After the close of the 1902 season, while the internecine warfare had still been going on, Crawford had signed a contract with the Detroit Tigers. When the coming truce appeared on the horizon, Sam signed another contract, with the Reds. As part of the peace treaty, however, it was determined that because Sam's contract with the Tigers predated his signing with the Reds, the star outfielder should be awarded to Detroit. So the Reds lost the man who for the next fifteen years would be one of the game's outstanding hitters.

Despite some solid hitting—the team's .288 batting average was the league's highest—Joe Kelley's 1903 Reds finished fourth. Outfielder Mike Donlin, who played just one full year for the Reds, batted .351, Cy Seymour .342, Beckley (who was sold to the Cardinals after the season) .327, and Steinfeldt .312. Seymour played some ramshackle defense, committing 36 errors, the all-time one-season record for a big-league outfielder. Hahn repeated his 22–12 record of the year before, completing every one of his 34 starts, helping the staff to a league-high 126 complete games. Skipper Kelley inserted himself into 105 games, playing infield and outfield, and batted .316.

Miller Huggins is remembered primarily as manager of 6 pennant-winning New York Yankee teams of the 1920s. But the little man—he was around 5 feet 5 inches tall—first made his name as a second baseman with the Reds.

Second base had been a headache for the Reds since McPhee's retirement, but when Huggins joined the club in 1904 the problem was solved. The twenty-five-year-old Huggins was joining his hometown team—he had been born in Cincinnati in 1879. He had studied law at the University of Cincinnati, but then succumbed to the lure of baseball. A .265 lifetime hitter, his strength was defense. (Nevertheless, on May 10, 1904, Miller hit Cincinnati's first grand-slam home run of the modern era. It was one of just 9 home runs he hit during his 13-year big-league career.)

Miller Huggins (1904–1909), looking more like the batboy than a twenty-five-year-old rookie second baseman.

With Kelley replacing Beckley at first base, Huggins at second, Corcoran at short, and Steinfeldt at third, the Reds had one of the league's better infields. Seymour's .313 average led the team.

After winning more than 20 games in 4 of his 5 big-league seasons, Hahn in 1904 dropped to 16–18. The truth was, the twenty-five-year-old ace was just about pitched out. An arm injury the following year (one story has him hurting himself experimenting with a spitball) brought his career with the Reds to an abrupt halt. He retired in 1906 after a few games with the Yankees.

With Hahn slipping, the ace of the staff was right-hander Jack Harper, who was 23–9, the best year of his career. Tom Walker and lefty Win Kellum, neither of whom lasted very long with the Reds, were 15-game winners. Right-hander Bob Ewing, who would have a long and productive career on the Cincinnati mound, was 11–13.

The 1904 club was 88–65, the best record for a Cincinnati team in the twentieth century until the pennant winners of 1919, but it was good enough only for third place, 18 games behind the pennant-winning Giants. John McGraw's New Yorkers were then the game's top drawing cards; a Reds-Giants game at Redland Field in early June attracted what was up to that time the largest crowd ever to watch a ball game: 37,223.

In 1905 the Reds slipped to fifth place, despite a thunderous season by Seymour. For Cy, always a dependable hitter, it was a year

Right-hander Jack Harper (1904–1906), who was 23–9 for the Reds in 1904.

fit for bronzing. The Reds outfielder won the batting championship with a .377 average and also led in hits (219), doubles (40), triples (21), runs batted in (121), total bases (325), and slugging (.559). Cy was just one home run short of a Triple Crown, with 8 circle shots to 9 for teammate Fred Odwell, which was enough to lead the league in those days of the short-traveling ball. (Odwell, an outfielder, was an unlikely home-run champ. In 1904, his first year in the majors, he hit only 1 and in two more seasons with the Reds

Bob Ewing, one of the Reds' most reliable pitchers during the first decade of the century.

Cy Seymour, whose .377 batting average in 1905 is still the highest in Reds history. Cy was with the Reds from 1902 to 1906.

he did not hit any. The Reds were not to produce another home-run leader until Ted Kluszewski in 1954.) Seymour's .377 average remains the team's record high, and Cy's 121 RBIs stood as the team standard until 1939 (no Reds player, in fact, was to drive in 100 runs again until George Kelly did it in 1929).

Bob Ewing with a 20–11 record was the staff leader, while newcomer Orval Overall was 17–22. The Reds misjudged the potential of Overall, and early the following season traded him to the Cubs, receiving little in return. In Chicago he became an ace pitcher, a mainstay on the staffs of four pennant winners in five years.

Herrmann made a managerial move after the 1905 season, replacing Kelley with Ned Hanlon. Ned had managed the famous Baltimore Orioles of the 1890s, where he had gained a reputation for daring and innovation (the Orioles reputedly were the first team to use the hit-and-run play and to perfect relays and rundowns). Kelley, who had been one of Hanlon's stars at Baltimore, remained with the Reds as an outfielder, his playing career just about at an end.

Hanlon's experience in Cincinnati proved once again that without talented players, managerial genius is a lot of shadow boxing. Seymour, who the previous year had scorched league pitching, was hitting .257 in early July when he was sold to the Giants. Steinfeldt had been traded to the Cubs for left-hander

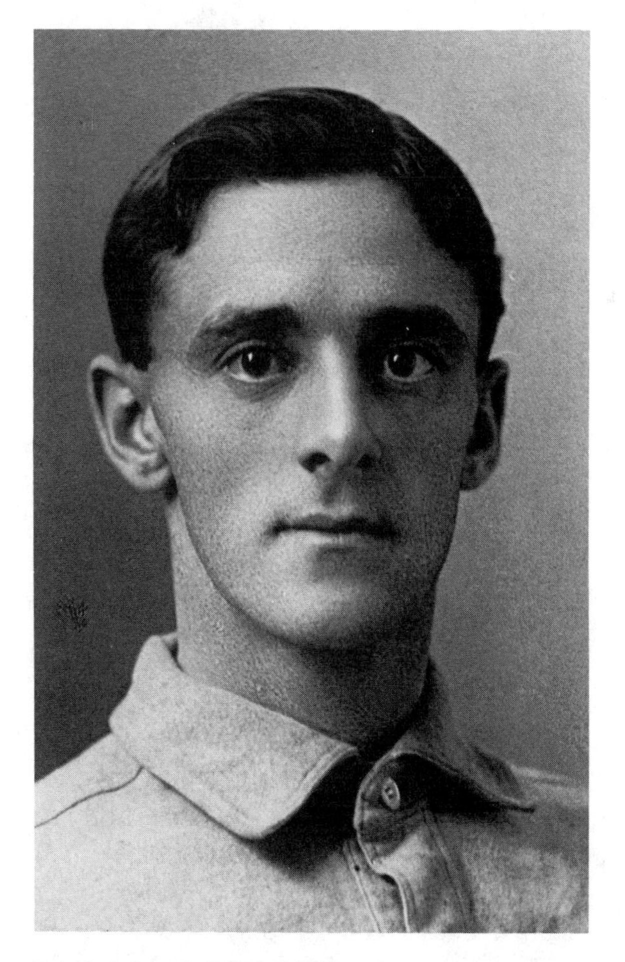

Fred Odwell (1904–1907), whose 9 home runs in 1905 led the league.

Orval Overall (1905–1906), a talented right-hander the Reds let get away.

Jake Weimer and infielder Hans Lobert. Weimer, whose fastball had earned him the nickname "Tornado Jake," was 20–14 for the Reds. Lobert got into 79 games and batted .310. A congenial man who was blessed with terrific running speed, Hans once explained the origin of his nickname.

"It was because of Wagner," he said. "He was known sometimes as Honus and sometimes as Hans. Well, people said we looked somewhat alike. Same big noses, anyway. We were both Dutchman, both infielders, both had John for a first name. The only little difference between us was that he could hit, run, throw, and field better than I could. Better than anybody could, for that matter."

Hanlon brought the club in sixth in 1906 and again in 1907, with almost identical records: 64–87 in 1906 and 66–87 in 1907. The 1906 club finished 51½ games out of first place, which in baseball calculations amounts to light-years.

Weimer, 1906's big winner, dropped to 11–14 in 1907 and was soon gone. Ewing was 17–19 and right-hander Andy Coakley, in his only full season with the Reds, was 17–16. Outfielder Mike Mitchell led the hitters with a .292 average, while rookie catcher Larry McLean batted .289. The club's regular catcher until 1912, McLean was at six feet, five inches a giant of a man among ball players of the time. Amiable when sober, the big man could be belligerent when drinking, and his career was marked by a series of vi-

George Schlei; nicknamed "Admiral," caught for the Reds from 1904 through 1908.

Ned Hanlon, who managed the Reds in 1906 and 1907.

Hans Lobert (1906–1910), the speedy infielder, who batted .310 in his rookie year.

Lefty Jake Weimer (1906–1908) was 20–14 in 1906.

Catcher Larry McLean (1906–1912), amiable when sober. Liquor sent tempests through him, and he ended up shot to death on a barroom floor in 1921.

Outfielder Mike Mitchell (1907–1912), who led the league in triples in 1909 and 1910.

John Ganzel (1907–1908) led in triples in 1907 and managed the Reds in 1908.

Outfielder Dode Paskert (1907–1910, 1921). The blur under his right arm tells us Dode missed this batting practice rip.

Right-hander Bob Spade (1907–1910) was 17–12 in 1908, his only big year.

olent confrontations that finally frayed the patience of his employers and brought his departure from the big leagues in 1915, when he was with the Giants. A drink-sodden McLean had had the temerity to challenge manager John McGraw and some friends to a fight, the episode ending with Larry having a chair smashed over his head. He died in 1921 in a Boston barroom when an irate bartender pumped a couple of pistol shots into the rampaging ex-catcher.

A dispirited Hanlon handed in his ticket after the 1907 season. Ned was succeeded by the club's first baseman, John Ganzel, whose unhappy lot it was to preside over the weakest hitting club in Reds history. With Lobert (.293) the only man to bat over .250, the team logged all-time Cincinnati lows for batting average (.227), runs (488), hits (1,108), and home runs (14, tied by the 1916 club).

Feathery hitting was the norm in the league in 1908 (the collective average of .239 remains the lowest in National League history), and despite their modest offense the Reds managed to finish fifth. In his only big year for the club, rookie right-hander Bob Spade was 17–12 and the dependable Ewing was 17–15.

Second baseman Dick Egan (1908–1913).

Clark Griffith, Cincinnati manager from 1909 to 1911.

But the 1908 season was not a complete washout for the Reds; they introduced several new young players who would help brighten future summer afternoons at Redland Field: speedy outfielder Bob Bescher, first baseman Dick Hoblitzell, and second baseman Dick Egan.

Ganzel was bounced as manager after the 1908 season and was replaced by Clark Griffith. Later known as the long-time owner of the Washington Senators, Griffith had been a winning pitcher in the National League in the 1890s, jumped to the newly formed American League in 1901 as pitcher-manager of the Chicago White Sox, and later managed New York's entry in the new league.

Griffith brought the club in fourth in 1909, creating enough interest for the Reds to set a new club attendance record of 424,643. The fans liked the style of Hoblitzell, who batted .308; Egan, who replaced Miller Huggins at second base; and Bescher, who although batting only .240, led the league with 54 stolen bases. Mike Mitchell hit a team-high .310 and hit a league-high 17 triples.

Jack Rowan (1908–1910, 1913–1914), whose best was 14–13 in 1910.

Art Fromme (1909–1913) was 19–13 in 1909.

Right-hander Art Fromme, obtained in a trade with the Cardinals, was the club's big winner with a 19–13 record, followed by rookie righty Harry Gaspar, who was 18–11.

The 1910 club came in fifth. Fromme was ineffective, winning only three games, with the slack being picked up by newcomer George Suggs, a right-hander who was 19–11. Mitchell again was tops in triples (18), and Bescher repeated as stolen base leader, setting a new league record with 70 swipes.

So the first decade of baseball's modern era ended with the Reds mired in the middle of the league, unable to compete successfully with the Giants, Cubs, and Pirates, who between them had taken all ten of the pennants won between 1901 and 1910. Things would get better, but first they would get worse.

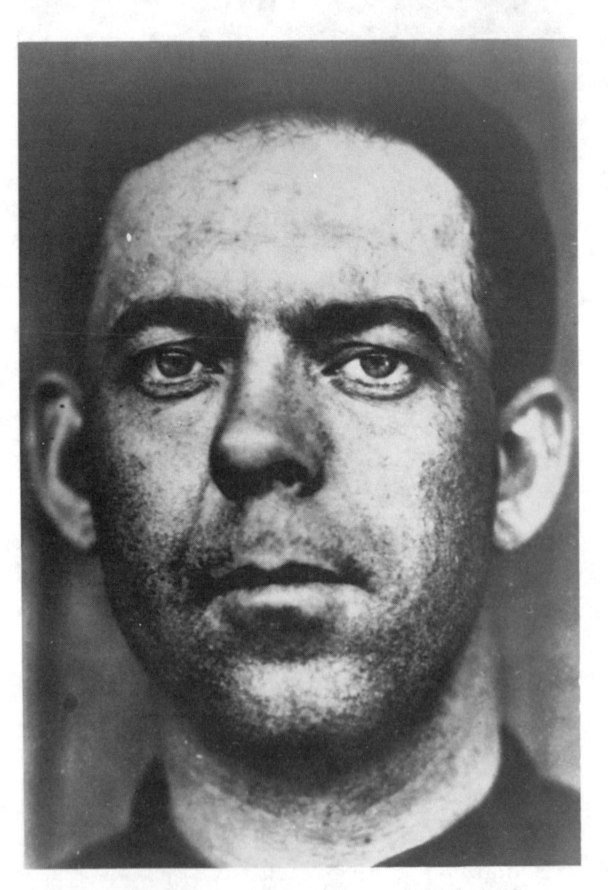

This rugged mug belongs to right-hander Harry Gaspar (1909–1912), who was 18–11 in his rookie year.

F·I·V·E

MOVING TOWARD THE TOP

THE Reds began the new decade pretty much as they had finished the old—in sixth place. Griffith's top hitter that year was outfielder Johnny Bates (.292), who had been acquired from the Phillies in a eight-player deal that saw Lobert go to Philadelphia. The team was last in home runs with 21, and 11 of those were hit by Hoblitzell. With a 15–13 record, Suggs again led the staff.

First baseman Dick Hoblitzell (1908–1914), whose top year was .308 in 1909.

Outfielder Johnny Bates (1911–1914).

For the third straight year Bescher was the stolen base leader, this time with 81. Still the single-season high for a Cincinnati team, it remained the league pinnacle until 1962, when Maury Wills shattered all records with his landmark 104 steals.

The Reds also enlisted what in 1911 was a bit of exotica for their fans—Cuban players. Although blacks were still unwelcome in

Outfielder Ward Miller (1909–1910). His 11 pinch hits led the league in 1910. The man just behind him is Dick Hoblitzell, with Larry McLean on the far right.

organized ball, light-skinned Latins were allowed, although few made it to the big leagues in those days. The Reds bought third baseman Rafael Almeida and outfielder Armando Marsans from the New Britain club of the Connecticut League. Neither played very much in 1911, and Almeida's career was brief, but Marsans became a regular the next year.

The highlight of the Reds' 1911 season came on June 4, when the club set an all-time scoring record for a Cincinnati team, shelling the Braves by a score of 26–3.

Champion base stealer Bob Bescher (1908–1913) led the league in steals for four straight seasons, with his 81 in 1911 still the club record.

Wearing the very latest in equipment is Tommy Clarke, who caught for the Reds from 1909 through 1917.

George Suggs (1910–1913) was a 19-game winner in 1910 and again in 1912. He jumped to the Federal League in 1914.

Infielder Tom Downey (1909–1911).

(RIGHT) Hank Severeid, a backup catcher for the Reds from 1911 to 1913 who later had a long and successful career in the American League.

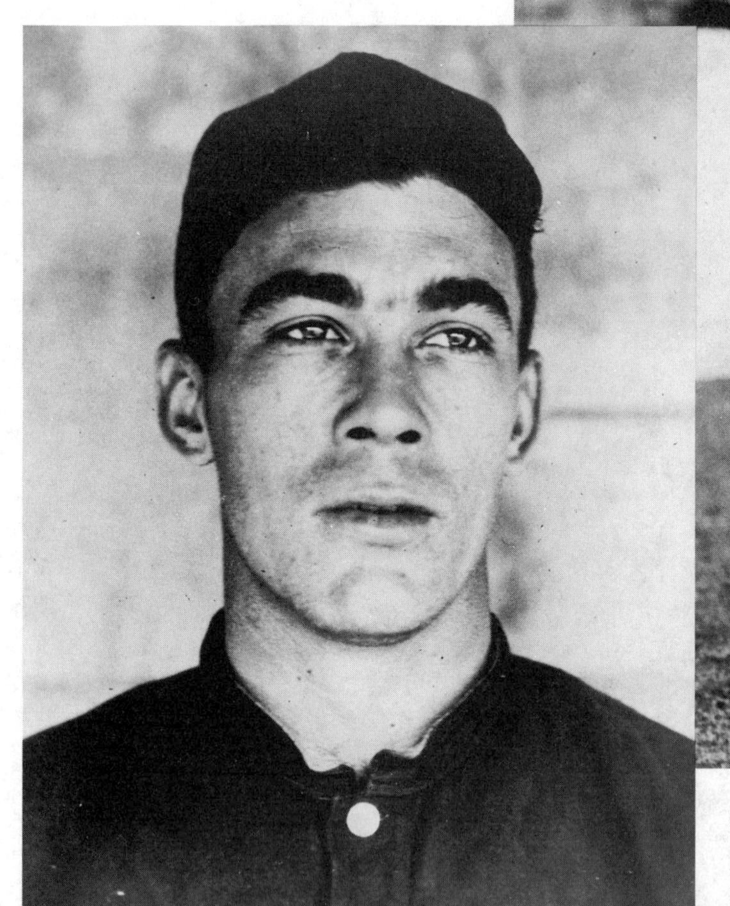

(LEFT) Outfielder Armando Marsans (1911–1914), one of big-league ball's first Cuban-born players. He batted .317 in 1912 and joined the Federal League in 1914.

The Reds were also involved in the game that closed down what is perhaps the most remarkable career of any big-league pitcher. On September 30, they defeated the forty-four-year-old Cy Young, 4–1, in what was the living legend's final game. Young, who had come to the major leagues in 1890 and was now wrapping it up with the Braves, left behind a mammoth 511–313 lifetime record. The man who beat him was young southpaw Rube Benton, who would carve out a long and respectable career for himself.

After three years and three progressively worse finishes—fourth, fifth, and sixth—Griffith was dismissed as manager and replaced by Hank O'Day. Hank was about as singular a character as ever labored in the big-league vineyards, with a career to match his eccentric personality. He was crusty and taciturn, to the point that one of his contemporaries described him as "damn near unapproachable." In an age when hotel lobby sitting was an art form among ball players, it was said that the silent O'Day could outlast the potted plants around him.

O'Day had come to the big leagues as a

pitcher in 1884, working in the American Association, National League, and finally in the Players' League, retiring in 1890 at the age of twenty-eight. He returned to the National League in 1895 as an umpire, the job he left to take over as skipper of the Reds. Hank managed the Reds for just one year, managed the Cubs for one year (1914), and then returned to umpiring, retiring for keeps in 1927.

After a devastating fire ravaged Redland Field in 1911, Herrmann had it rebuilt with concrete and steel. The new structure, which remained the home of the Reds until the erection of Riverfront Stadium in 1970, greeted Cincinnati fans on opening day 1912.

Perhaps inspired by their bright new surroundings, the Reds won 20 of their first 25 games in 1912, but then began a slide that saw them finish fourth. Marsans led the team with a surprising .317 mark, and Bescher swiped 67 bases for a fourth straight league leadership.

O'Day ran three strong-armed pitchers through the league: Suggs was 19–16, Benton 18–21, and Fromme 16–18. Between them, they started 112 of the team's 154 games.

Soon after the season's close, Herrmann dismissed O'Day and then went about swinging a trade to obtain his new skipper. On December 11, the Reds swapped outfielders Mike Mitchell and Pete Knisley, infielders Red Corriden and Art Phelan, and pitcher Bert Humpheries to the Cubs for catcher Harry Chapman, pitcher Grover Lowdermilk, and shortstop Joe Tinker.

Tinker was the man Herrmann coveted, not so much to play—the thirty-two-year-old shortstop's playing days were almost over—as to manage. Herrmann believed that the one-time lead man on baseball's most famous double-play combination was just the man to turn things around in Cincinnati.

Tinker turned things around all right, but in the wrong direction—the club sank to seventh place, despite a .317 season from the skipper. The best thing to happen to the Reds in 1913 was a trade they made with the Giants on May 22. Off to New York went Art Fromme and infielder Eddie Grant (who was later killed in action in the Argonne Forest near the end of World War I) and to Cincinnati came right-hander Red Ames, outfielder Josh Devore, and second baseman Heinie Groh. The pick of the group turned out to be Groh. The twenty-three-year-old Groh, who had seen little action under McGraw, would soon be moved to third base, where he was to excel for the Reds until 1920. With his arrival, the Reds now had in place the first member of the team that would bring Cincinnati its first pennant in 1919.

Hank O'Day, Cincinnati's manager in 1912.

Joe Tinker, Cincinnati's shortstop-manager in 1913. His .317 batting average that year is the highest ever for a Cincinnati shortstop.

Pitching for the Reds that year was Mordecai ("Three Finger") Brown. One of pitching's noblest thoroughbreds when he was with the Cubs in the previous decade, Brown had been released by Chicago and acquired by the Reds. Playing for his old shortstop buddy Tinker, Three Finger had enough left to crank out an 11–12 season.

When Herrmann decided to change managers he again took the trade route. The man Garry wanted was Giants infielder Buck Herzog, known as one of the game's shrewder players. To get Herzog, Herrmann sent the Giants his wing-footed outfielder Bob Bescher.

Herzog's tenure as Reds manager, which lasted until midway through the 1916 season, proved to be a dismal one. The 1914 club finished in the cellar with a 60–94 record. Worse, the team's home attendance sank to an all-time low of 100,791. Capping a wretched summer, in September the Reds set a team record with 19 straight losses, the third longest tailspin in modern National League history. Only Groh (.288) and Herzog (.281)—the club's second manager-shortstop in two years—showed any respectability at bat. Ames (15–23) and Benton (17–18) labored heroically throughout the season.

If the 1914 season wasn't bad enough for the Reds on the field, a misguided scouting trip made it even worse. According to Lee Allen, who tells the story in his splendid history of the Reds, Herrmann sent a friend named Harry Stevens to scout the Baltimore Orioles, then of the International League. The Reds at the time had a working agreement

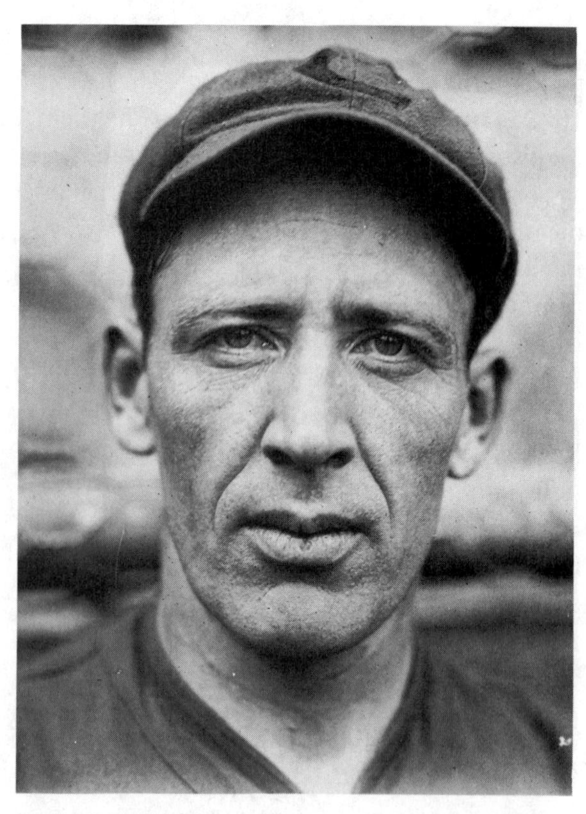

Right-hander Leon ("Red") Ames (1913–1915). His 23 losses led the league in 1914.

with Baltimore the terms of which allowed them to select any two of the Oriole players. Stevens, who had no apparent qualifications for such an assignment, watched the Orioles play and then made his choices: shortstop Claud Derrick, who played just two games for the Reds, and outfielder George Twombly, who got into 68 games and batted .233. Stevens managed to overlook Baltimore left-hander Babe Ruth.

"Not many teams," a wistful Cincinnati fan said years later, "can say they traded Mathewson and overlooked Ruth."

Cincinnati's problems in 1914 were part of a larger cloud that had settled over the National and American Leagues. Reminiscent of the bad old days, a new major league had been formed, the Federal League. This confection began as a most formidable challenge to the established leagues; emboldened by an array of well-heeled owners, the Feds began

The great Mordecai ("Three Finger") Brown (1913, 1916) arrived in Cincinnati with too little and too late.

Buck Herzog (1914–1916), Cincinnati's shortstop-manager.

raiding the big-league rosters like so many genteel buccaneers. They attracted enough talent to field an 8-team league in 1914 and another in 1915, after which spotty attendance and failing franchises brought the league to collapse.

The Reds, who were fortunate not to have a Federal League team planted in their city (Pittsburgh, St. Louis, Chicago, and Brooklyn suffered through two seasons with unwelcome neighbors) had only minimal losses to the predatory Federals: outfielder Armando Marsans and pitcher George Johnson, who had won 14 games in 1913. Three Finger Brown also jumped to the new league, but the old pitcher was by now at the far end of the string.

Outfielder Tommy Griffith (1915–1918) gave the Reds a .307 year in 1915.

On the face of it, the Reds did little better in 1915, finishing up a notch in seventh, but actually it was much better, for the club played as well as any seventh-place team ever has, posting a 71–83 record (only the seventh-place 1917 Brooklyn Dodgers, with a 70–81 record have done better in that lowly slot).

Outfielder Tommy Griffith led the team with a .307 average and right-hander Gene Dale, in his only full season with the team, was 18–17. The top pitcher, however, was right-hander Fred Toney, who had had several trials with the Cubs before being acquired by the Reds. Although not making his first start until early June, Toney went on to a 15–6 record and 1.58 ERA, second best in the league that year and lowest ever for a Cincinnati pitcher.

With the collapse of the Federal League in 1915, some talented players became available, among them first baseman Hal Chase. The thirty-three-year-old Chase was one of

Fred Toney (1915–1918), victor in the famous "double no-hit" duel with Hippo Vaughn in 1917, the year Fred won 24 games for the Reds.

the most famous ball players in the country, with opinions of him ranging from awe to contempt. He had come to the big leagues with the New York Yankees (then known as the Highlanders) in 1905 and quickly established a reputation as the most dazzling defensive first baseman the game had ever seen. A steady if unspectacular hitter, Chase, who soon had the nickname "Prince Hal," was so magical with his glove that he became a fans' favorite and the first of the many great drawing cards to play for the New York club.

The other side of Hal Chase was bathed in shadows. He was, everyone agreed, a man's man, one who was handy with his fists, could ride a horse, was a crack shot, could hold his liquor, and who possessed considerable charm. He was also a gambler, and among his friends were many who inhabited New York's shadier precincts. Chase was soon suspected of betting on games in which he participated, and the bets were not always on his own side. There were a lot of suspicious maneuvers around first base. "He was so quick around the bag," one teammate said, "that he could muck up an easy play and make it look like it was nobody's fault."

Chase's ambiguous performances, along with the growing odor emanating from his reputation, moved the Yankees to get rid of him, trading him to the White Sox. Shortly after, he jumped to the Federal League. So compelling were his talents, that despite Chase's reputation, when the Federal League collapsed, Garry Herrmann signed him.

In 1916, his first year with the Reds, Chase batted a career-high .339, which was good enough to lead the league.

With the Reds wallowing in the cellar after 83 games, Herrmann decided it was again time to change managers, and once more he obtained his new skipper through a trade, although this time the man he got was at the end of his career.

On July 20, 1916, the Reds traded their shortstop-manager Buck Herzog along with outfielder Red Killefer to the Giants for Christy Mathewson, journeyman infielder Bill McKechnie, and outfielder Edd Roush.

Hal Chase (1916–1918): charming, talented, notorious.

Mathewson's long and distinguished career had about wound down, and when Christy was offered the opportunity to manage, McGraw gave his greatest pitcher and personal favorite the chance. In hiring Mathewson, Herrmann was succumbing to what baseball people before and since have—the aura of the aging superstar, the rather romantic hope that a titan of the past can somehow suffuse a club with the glow of his old magic.

Although no one could have known it at the time, in making the trade the Reds acquired the man who, until the coming of Frank Robinson forty years later, was re-

Newly arrived from New York *(left to right):* Bill McKechnie, new manager Christy Mathewson, and Edd Roush. McKechnie, who played for the Reds in 1916–1917, later returned as a long-time manager.

garded as the greatest player in franchise history.

Edd Roush was twenty-three years old at the time of the trade. The left-handed hitting native of Oakland City, Indiana, had played briefly with the White Sox in 1913, then jumped to the Federal League for two years before signing with the Giants in 1916. He batted .188 in 39 games for McGraw before the usually keen-eyed skipper let him slip away, although it probably wasn't entirely a McGraw misjudgment—the two men never cared much for one another.

A swift, sure-handed center fielder (he was known as the "Tris Speaker of the National League," which in those days was the accolade of accolades for an outfielder), the individualistic Roush became known as much for his stubbornness at the bargaining table as for his methodic hitting. A man with a very precise sense of his own worth, Roush in 1922 sat out half the season until the Reds saw the figures his way.

Roush had another reason for his perennial holdouts. In Lawrence Ritter's warm and insightful classic *The Glory of Their Times,* Edd told Ritter, "I used to hold out every year until the week before the season opened. That's the only time they ever had any trouble with me, contract time. Why should I go down there and fuss around in spring training? Twist an ankle, or break a leg. I did my *own* spring training, hunting quail and rabbits around Oakland City."

Much to the disappointment of Reds fans, Mathewson had announced upon taking over as manager that his playing days were over (he had been just 3–4 with the Giants). However, it was further announced that on September 4 Matty would take the mound for one last game, his opponent being Three Finger Brown, who was spooning out the last drops of his career now with the Cubs.

The game was promoted excitedly in the Cincinnati papers and for one last time the National League's two mightiest pitchers of the previous decade went head to head. In a sentiment-drenched game, each former ace went the distance and demonstrated that the passage of time had left certain things irreversible: Matty labored to an embarrassing 15-hit, 10–8 victory. (This sentimental "duel" was to burn itself in the record books, however. The victory was Mathewson's 373d and last; years later Grover Cleveland Alexander, after climbing to a similar 373 lifetime victories could go no further, leaving the two majestic aces forever tied at the top of the league's victory scroll.)

Mathewson's magic was unable to inspire the team, and at season's end the club was in last place, despite a .254 batting average that was second best in the league. After Chase, the club's top hitter was Roush, who batted .287 in 69 games.

Sizing up his club, Mathewson decided the first order of business was strengthening the pitching. With Chase, Groh, shortstop Larry Kopf, catcher Ivy Wingo, and outfielders

Shortstop Larry Kopf (1916–1917, 1919–1921).

Catcher Ivy Wingo, who enjoyed a long career with the Reds (1915–1926, 1929).

Roush, Earle ("Greasy") Neale, and Tommy Griffith, the club was solid. Matty had two reliable starters in Toney and right-hander Pete Schneider, but they were not enough. So the skipper began filtering into the rotation left-handers Hod Eller and Dutch Ruether and right-hander Jimmy Ring, each young and talented, creating the basis for what would soon be a strong pitching staff.

Pitching was never better than on the afternoon of May 2, 1917. It was on this day that Toney and the Cubs' Jim ("Hippo") Vaughn went at it in one of those one-of-a-kind games with which baseball occasionally thrills and delights its fans.

It was a chilly afternoon at Chicago's Weeghman Field (today's Wrigley Field), with about 3,000 fans on hand. They got their money's worth, for after nine innings not only was there no score but neither pitcher had allowed a hit, making it a game unprecedented (and thus far unduplicated) in major-

Earle ("Greasy") Neale (1916–1922, 1924), outfielder for the Cincinnati Reds and later coach for the Philadelphia Eagles.

league history. The spell was finally broken in the top of the tenth, when Kopf singled to right. After another out, Chase lifted a fly ball that center fielder Cy Williams dropped, putting men on first and third. Then Jim Thorpe, the former Olympic athlete, rolled one along the third base line that Vaughn fielded and fed to catcher Art Wilson, who misplayed it, allowing Kopf to score what was to be the only run of the game. Toney wove another inning of magic in the bottom of the tenth and completed his no-hit victory. The game sent Toney and Vaughn into baseball legend in eternal tandem, like Thomson and Branca and a handful of other memorable winners and losers.

The Reds had acquired Thorpe from the Giants in April. The famous Oklahoma-born Native American had made history with a stunning sweep of gold medals at the 1912 Olympic Games in Stockholm and was now trying his hand at big-league baseball. Despite his physical strength and mercurial speed afoot, the world's greatest athlete had trouble with the curveball and never made it in the majors. After batting .247 in 77 games for the Reds in 1917, he was dealt back to the Giants. He retired in 1919, a .252 lifetime hitter.

Jim Thorpe (1917). The world's greatest athlete had trouble with the curveball.

Right-hander Pete Schneider (1914–1918) was 20–19 in 1917.

"He was the strongest man I ever knew," Jimmy Ring said of Thorpe. "I roomed with him for a while. He liked to drink and he'd often come back to the room at night all lit up. When he was like that he wanted to wrestle. I had no choice but to wrestle with him. Now, I was a big strong guy myself, but he'd bounce me all over the place. Then he'd laugh and go to sleep. He was a good-natured guy, and I liked him, but he was a pain in the ass to room with."

Fred Toney, winner of the double no-hitter, had by no means exhausted his store of heroics in that game; on July 1 the 6-foot, 6-inch right-hander pitched and won both ends of a doubleheader against the Pirates, by scores of 4–1 and 5–1.

With Toney posting a 24–16 record, Pete Schneider at 20–19, and young Hod Eller 10--5, Mathewson was able to bring the club in fourth in 1917. (Toney's 7 shutouts tied the team record set by Jake Weimer in 1906; it was tied again by Eller in 1919 and by Jack Billingham in 1973.)

For the second year in a row the Reds had the batting champion, Roush logging the league's gaudiest average with a .341 mark, the first of 10 straight years in which Edd would hit substantially greater than .300. The Reds, in fact, had the league's highest team batting average (.264), although Groh at .304 was the only other .300 hitter on the squad.

World War I, which the United States had entered in April 1917, did not begin to impinge on baseball until the following season. In June 1918, the provost marshall issued what in effect was "a work or fight" order. This directive stipulated that all able-bodied men of draft age had to either enter the military or else join some essential, war-related industry. Another edict from Washington, this one from the secretary of war, directed that the baseball season be curtailed on September 2 (a period of grace was allowed for the playing of the World Series). The Reds played 129 games that year, which was about the average for most major-league clubs.

Among the Cincinnati players to join industry or the military were outfielder Pat Duncan, shortstop Larry Kopf, and pitchers Dutch Ruether and Rube Bressler. On August 27, 1918, the club lost its skipper to the war when Mathewson resigned to accept a captain's commission in the Chemical Warfare Branch of the U.S. Army. (Groh ran the team for the handful of games remaining.)

Before they lost their manager, the Reds also lost their enigmatic first baseman, although not because of the war. Aware of Chase's reputation, Mathewson had been watching him carefully and liking less and less of what he saw. Too many games were being lost because of a Chase misplay, some of them extremely subtle. Finally acting on his suspicion that his gifted first baseman was throwing games, Mathewson conferred with Herrmann, who then issued a statement that Chase was suspended without pay. This was on August 8; less than three weeks later, Mathewson joined the army.

Amid all of this, the Reds achieved a third-place finish, at that point their best of the modern era, despite having sold Toney to the Giants in July. The club again led the league in batting (.278), thanks to a .333 average from Roush and .320 from Groh. Eller was the big winner with a 16–12 record.

After the close of the season, Herrmann brought formal charges of throwing games against Chase. League president John Heydler presided over the hearings. The club's case against Chase was weakened by the unavoidable absence of his chief accuser, Mathewson, who was by then in France. Affidavits from Matty were presented, but they lacked the weight and moral authority his physical presence would have added.

Despite his own misgivings, Heydler, partially because he thought the case was not strong enough and partially in fear of the adverse publicity banishment would bring, acquitted Chase.

(Curiously, Chase was signed in 1919 by John McGraw to play for the Giants. The dictatorial John J. apparently believed he could control the talented, but devious, Chase. He couldn't: Before the end of the season Prince Hal was quietly dropped by the Giants and at the age of thirty-six left organized ball forever, leaving behind a reputation as, in the words of one writer, "Baseball's Benedict Arnold.")

S·I·X

THE MOST FAMOUS WORLD SERIES

THE 1919 World Series remains the most minutely examined and thoroughly chronicled of all baseball's postseason pageants. It has generated legends and controversies, even a movie (*Eight Men Out,* based on Eliot Asinof's definitive book on the subject). Unfortunately, the team that won the 1919 World Series—the Cincinnati Reds—is long gone and little remembered, overshadowed by a band of Chicago White Sox players whose ethics vaporized at a crucial moment. The emphasis on that World Series has always been so relentlessly focused it almost seems as if only one team played in it. But as far as the Reds were concerned, their feelings on the subject were summed up years later by their tough right-hander Jimmy Ring, who had developed his fastball on the sandlots of Maspeth, Long Island: "We would have beaten them anyway."

January 1919 was a worrying time for Garry Herrmann; the Hal Chase hearings had been held and now the Reds president was wondering about his manager. The war was over and Christy Mathewson was still in France, with Herrmann unable to contact him to see when, or indeed if, Matty would return as manager. After a series of cables went unanswered, Herrman had no choice but to look elsewhere. The man he found was Pat Moran.

Formerly a catcher with the Braves, Cubs, and Phillies, the forty-three-year-old Moran had switched to managing after the close of his 14-year playing career. In his first shot at

Fastballer Jimmy Ring (1917–1920).

Pat Moran, who managed the Reds from 1919 through 1923.

dugout brainstorming, Pat had in 1915 managed the Phillies to their first pennant and followed up that success with a pair of second-place finishes. After a sixth-place windup in 1918, Pat resigned because of disagreements with the front office. Now he was taking over the Reds, their tenth manager since 1901.

The club that Moran put together that spring looked like this: Jake Daubert, first base; Morrie Rath, second base; Larry Kopf, shortstop; Heinie Groh, third base; Ivy Wingo and Bill Rariden, catchers; Edd Roush and Greasy Neale the outfield regulars, with several other players alternating as the third outfielder. (This was the same Greasy Neale who coached the Philadelphia Eagles to the National Football League championship in 1949.)

Daubert, known as "Gentleman Jake" for his courtly demeanor and snappy wardrobe, had put in nine fine years with Brooklyn, where he had won two batting crowns. When Jake asked his employer Charlie Ebbets for more money than Charlie wanted to pay, he found himself traded to Cincinnati for outfielder Tommy Griffith.

Moran's Reds were a good if unspectacular club; where they excelled was on the mound. Here the skipper found himself with an enviable array of starters in left-handers Harry ("Slim") Sallee and Dutch Ruether, and righties Hod Eller, Jimmy Ring, and Ray Fisher. In addition, the club had the first of the truly outstanding Cubans to come to the major leagues in curveballing right-hander Dolf Luque.

Sallee, an eleven-year veteran, had been obtained from the Giants via the waiver route, and the thirty-four-year-old southpaw proved to be a great bargain. Fisher, another veteran—he had spent eight years in the American League with the Yankees—was also acquired on waivers and he, too, delivered more than had been expected.

Cincinnati's year of glory began on a dismal note. Moran took the team to Waxahachie, Texas, for spring training and immediately encountered days and days of rain. The playing field, located in one of the lowest parts of the city, was constantly flooded, forcing the team to take their workouts where they could, and their improvised playing areas included a cow pasture, the railroad yards, various empty lots, and even the cemetery. When the club broke camp and began barnstorming their way home, they ran into more rain and were able to play just a handful of games. But once the season opened, the team played as if to prove Edd Roush's dictum that spring training was su-

The infield of the 1919 National League pennant winners *(left to right):* third baseman Heinie Groh, shortstop Larry Kopf, second baseman Morrie Rath, first baseman Jake Daubert.

perfluous—if you had kept yourself in decent shape. (Edd, as was his wont, had missed the Waxahachie fun by staging one of his holdouts, which he ended, as he usually did, just before the opening of the season.)

The Reds surprised everybody by winning their first seven games in 1919. It soon became obvious that Cincinnati's pitching was going to keep them in the race all summer. With five starters and Luque a talented sixth, Moran was able to keep his pitchers fresh. On May 11, Eller thrilled the fans at Redland Field by no-hitting the Cardinals, 6–0.

Eller featured a freak delivery known as a "shine ball," a pitch that broke sharply as it approached the plate. Hod was unwilling to divulge the secret behind his pitch, although what he probably did was put talcum powder on his pants' leg and smooth one side of the ball by rubbing it against the substance when he was on the mound, causing an eccentric spin and break. Doctoring a baseball was not

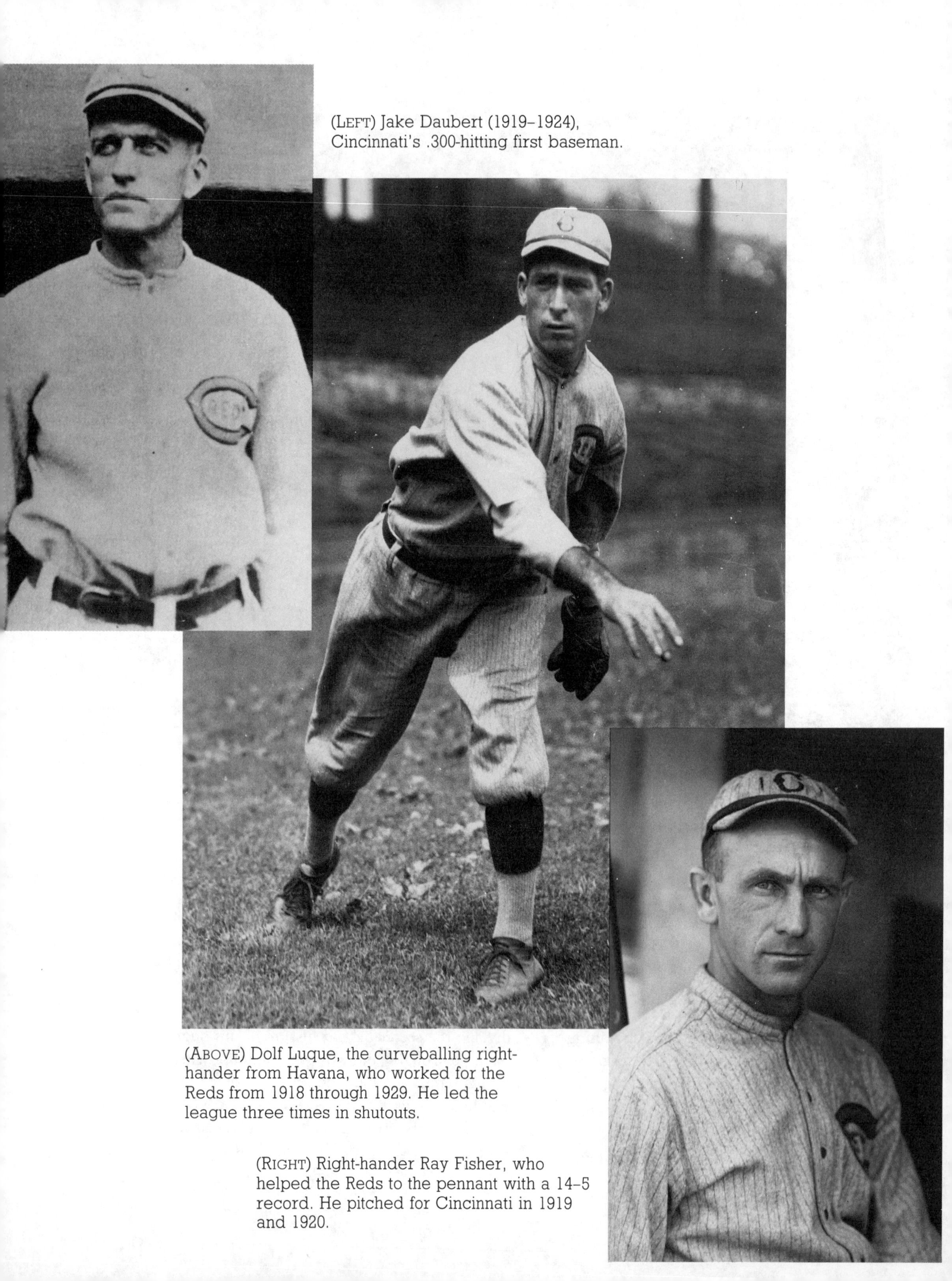

(LEFT) Jake Daubert (1919–1924), Cincinnati's .300-hitting first baseman.

(ABOVE) Dolf Luque, the curveballing right-hander from Havana, who worked for the Reds from 1918 through 1929. He led the league three times in shutouts.

(RIGHT) Right-hander Ray Fisher, who helped the Reds to the pennant with a 14–5 record. He pitched for Cincinnati in 1919 and 1920.

Hod Eller (1917–1921), exponent of the shine ball, was 20–9 in 1919.

yet illegal—the spitball was a favorite pitch then. But after the 1919 season a new rule forbade the doctoring of baseballs, and Eller, deprived of his best pitch, quickly lost his effectiveness.

After trailing the first-place Giants by five games on June 1, the Reds began winning steadily and hopped right on the tail of a strong McGraw-led team.

In mid-August the Reds came into New York to play the Giants three doubleheaders in three days. Moran's club swept the first, lost the second, and won the third, giving them first place. A 10-game winning streak in Boston, Brooklyn, and Philadelphia enabled them to build a 7-game lead by September 2. With the schedule having been limited to 140 games by club owners uncertain about the postwar economy, this lead was all but insurmountable.

On September 16, Ruether beat the Giants 4–3 at Redland Field and clinched Cincinnati's first pennant. With a season's record of 96–44, the Reds' final margin over the Giants was 9 games. With 532,501 turnstile spins that summer, the club set a new attendance mark.

In winning the final National League pennant of the dead ball era, Cincinnati's hitters, with one exception, did not light any offensive fires. The exception was Roush, whose .321 average was good enough to earn him his second batting title. The only other .300 hitter on the team was Groh (.310). Daubert, Kopf, and Wingo were at .270 or better. Overall, the team batted .263, second to New York's .269. The pennant winners popped just 20 home runs, with Groh's 5 the best. (The Phillies hit the most home runs: 42.)

Outfielder Sherry Magee (1917–1919) was the RBI leader in 1918.

Slim Sallee (1919–1920) was 21–7 in 1919.

Sallee gave the Reds the best of his 14 big-league seasons, a 21–7 record. Also turning in the top outings of their careers were Eller (20–9) and Ruether (19–6). Fisher was 14–5, Ring 10–9, and Luque 9–3. The staff's 2.23 ERA was second best to Chicago's 2.21, and their 23 shutouts led the league and set the all-time club record.

Going into their first World Series, the Reds were decided underdogs, their opponents a formidable Chicago White Sox club. The cream of the White Sox talent were outfielder "Shoeless Joe" Jackson, second baseman Eddie Collins, catcher Ray Schalk, and pitchers Eddie Cicotte and Lefty Williams. Other notables on the team were first baseman Chick Gandil, shortstop Swede Risberg, third baseman Buck Weaver, outfielder Happy Felsch, and pitchers Red Faber and Dickey Kerr.

As with any team, the White Sox were a diverse mix of personalities and backgrounds, ranging from the Columbia-educated Collins to the tough and sullen Gandil. There were two distinct factions on the squad, one that included Collins, Schalk, Kerr, and Faber, and another that centered around Gandil and Risberg and that included Cicotte, Williams, Felsch, Weaver, and the great hitter Jackson, who by all accounts was an affable and ingenuous man easily influenced by stronger personalities.

The latter contingent contained most of the club's malcontents, brooding over the parsimonious salaries dished out by their severely tight-fisted employer Charles Comiskey, the same Comiskey who had managed the Reds in the 1890s.

When the odds on the White Sox began dropping just before the Series opened, the pot began to boil.

"Rumors were flying all over the place that gamblers had got to the Chicago White Sox," Roush told Lawrence Ritter, "that they'd agreed to throw the World Series."

"There was too much smoke not to suspect some fire," Jimmy Ring said years later. "You couldn't help but hear the talk. Everybody knew something, but nobody knew everything. Moran told us to just go out and play our game and not pay attention. But don't think it didn't get to him, too. Just before the first game he told us, 'I know everybody here is clean, but if I see anything I don't like, the guy is right out of there.' "

The National Commission, in those pre-commissioner days still the game's ruling body, had decided to make the Series a 5-out-of-9 contest (this format remained in place for three years, reverting back to 4 of 7 in 1922). When the Series opened in Cincinnati on October 1, 1919, the odds had dropped to even money; but despite the thundercloud of rumors, most people were unwilling to believe that America's premier sporting event had been fixed.

The signal from the White Sox to the gamblers that the fix was in would come on the game's first batter: Cicotte would plunk leadoff man Morrie Rath with a pitch. When Rath was duly struck by one of Eddie's first deliveries, the gamblers winked at each other and sat back and relaxed.

The Reds ran off with the opener, Ruether beating Cicotte, 9–1, largely on the strength of a 5-run fourth inning that included some glaringly sloppy White Sox play.

After Sallee won Game 2, 4–2, the rumors took on more substance. Seven White Sox players, it would later be revealed, were in on the swindle: Cicotte, Williams, Gandil, Jackson, Felsch, Risberg, and utilityman Fred McMullin, who played very little but insisted on being included in the scheme when he happened to overhear it being planned. (One writer later described Fred as "a guilty bystander.") An eighth player, Weaver, did not participate in the fix, but knew about it and chose to say nothing, a stance that was to cost him his career.

Catcher Bill Rariden (1919–1920).

Left-hander Dutch Ruether (1917–1920), who gave the Reds a big 19–6 year in 1919.

The Series moved to Chicago for the third game, in which Kerr pitched a 3–0 shutout over Fisher to give the White Sox their first victory. (According to later stories, the fixers, who had not received all of their promised money, had gone all-out to win the game in order to send a message to the gamblers.)

Ring shut out the White Sox in Game 4,

TRIC CO. DYNAMOS
9 2 3 2
AT BAT STRIKES BALLS OUTS
TEAMS. 1 2 3 4 5 6 7 8 9 10 P. C.
CIN'TI 0 0 0 3 0 11 9
CHI'GO 0 0 0 0 0 0 14 8
UMPIRES
PLATE BASES
R.LINE 9 L.LINE 7
THIS SCORE BOARD
MAKE A HIT WITH—
Puritan
CINCINNATI

That's Heinie Groh crossing the plate and Pat Duncan at third base heading for home. They scored on a triple by Larry Kopf. The action took place in the fourth inning of Game 2 of the 1919 World Series.

beating Cicotte, 2–0. Both Cincinnati runs in the top of the fifth were tainted. Reds outfielder Pat Duncan hit one back to Cicotte, whose throw to first was wild, enabling Duncan to go to second. When Kopf singled to left, Cicotte deflected Jackson's throw home, allowing Duncan to score.

"Cicotte had no business near that ball," Ring said. "It was as obvious a play as they made in the whole Series."

In Game 5, Eller beat Williams 5–0, the Reds breaking it open with four runs in the top of the sixth, thanks to some shoddy outfield play by Felsch.

When the Series shifted back to Cincinnati for Game 6, Kerr (who earned himself the nickname "Honest Dickie" for his work in the Series) won in ten innings, 5–4, beating Ring in relief of Ruether.

Perhaps embarrassed by Kerr's success, or concerned now about the unsavory stories that were circulating, Cicotte and friends won Game 7, beating Sallee 4–1.

The whole sorry and sordid affair, with its lies, deceptions, errors, and misplays came to an end in Chicago in Game 8. In an atrocious first inning, the brilliant curveballer Williams threw nothing but batting-practice fastballs, which the Cincinnati batters devoured for 4 runs. Behind Eller, the Reds won it, 10–5, taking their first world championship.

It's the bottom of the sixth inning of Game 2 of the 1919 World Series. Cincinnati's Greasy Neale, attempting to steal second, is being tagged out by Chicago's Swede Risberg. Bent over watching from the mound is pitcher Lefty Williams.

Heinie Groh (1913–1921) showing off his "bottle bat."

When the scandal finally broke the following September, it had lasting repercussions for baseball. Concerned with growing public cynicism about the integrity of their game, the owners agreed to hire a commissioner of baseball, charged him with cleaning up the game, and invested him with almost limitless powers to do so. The man they chose was federal judge Kenesaw Mountain Landis, a man of severe and unforgiving temperament. Upon the evidence set before him, Landis barred forever from organized ball the seven Chicago White Sox conspirators and added Weaver to the toll because of the latter's failure to report the fix.

The 1919 World Series has long been dominated by the story of the notorious White Sox (who have been handed down to history

Second baseman Morrie Rath (1919–1920).

as "The Black Sox"), leaving the winners in a sort of limbo.

"One thing that's always overlooked in the whole mess is that we could have beat them no matter what the circumstances." That was Edd Roush speaking, and probably from the heart.

Lest this talk seem purely chauvinistic, it was the astute Eddie Collins who a few years later told teammate Ted Lyons that by no means would even a dedicated White Sox team have had an easy time of it in the 1919 Series.

"That club had an abundance of good pitching," Collins said of the Reds, "and they played outstanding defense."

Collins was correct on both counts: the 1919 Reds tied a National League record for fewest errors (152) and set a new major-league record with a .974 fielding average.

So the 1919 Cincinnati Reds slipped into history, the only team that has ever had to defend their right to a world championship. One thing, however, had been justly earned, without any ambiguities—that cherished first pennant. Reds fans hoped they wouldn't have to wait another nineteen years for the next one. Well, they wouldn't. They would have to wait twenty.

Edd Roush (1916–1926, 1931). From 1917 through 1926 he never batted less than .320.

S·E·V·E·N

FAST START, SLOW FINISH

IN 1919, the National League batted .258; for the next decade the league would *average* .285. The era of the lively ball had begun, though Cincinnati's entrance into it was rather modest—just 18 home runs and a .277 batting average in 1920. (Actually, it was not until the 1950s that the Reds became a long ball–hitting team.)

The World Champions fielded a stand-pat team in 1920: Daubert, Rath, Kopf, and Groh again comprised the infield, Wingo was behind the plate, and the outfield was Roush, Neale, and Duncan. Moran's fine pitching

Heinie Groh.

Bubbles Hargrave (1921–1928), a catcher with a .300 stick who led the league in batting in 1926, one of only two catchers to do so.

staff also remained unchanged, with Eller, Ring, Ruether, Fisher, Sallee, and Luque the principal members.

As the season wore on, however, it became apparent that the Reds pitching was not as masterly as it had been the year before. Deprived of his shine ball by the new rule banning doctored baseballs, Eller lost much of his effectiveness, while the years suddenly caught up to Sallee (he was waived to the Giants in early September).

Despite some spotty pitching, the Reds were in a three-team race throughout much of the summer with the Giants and a surprising Dodger team. The Reds bobbed in and out of first place, holding the top spot as late as Labor Day, but then faltered on an eastern swing and slowly slipped to third, where they finished, 10½ games behind the Dodgers.

Roush hit .339 in 1920 and Daubert .304. Ring led the staff with a 17–16 record, followed by Ruether's 16–12. The team's good showing in 1920, plus the carry-over elation

Second baseman Lew Fonseca (1921–1924) batted .361 in 91 games in 1922.

Infielder Sammy Bohne (1921–1926). His top year was .285 in 1921.

from 1919 combined to attract a new attendance mark of 568,107.

Herrmann and Moran agreed that some retooling was necessary, and they set to work in the off-season. To shore up the catching, they purchased minor-league catcher Eugene ("Bubbles") Hargrave, who had flunked earlier trials with the Cubs but who now seemed ready. The contracts of minor-league infielders Lew Fonseca and Sammy Bohne were also acquired (Bohne was to replace Rath at second base).

The off-season also saw the dismantling of the championship pitching staff. Ruether was traded to the Dodgers for veteran left-hander Rube Marquard, and Ring was swapped, along with Neale, to the Phillies for left-hander Eppa Rixey. In addition, Fisher retired to take the job as baseball coach at the University of Michigan. So of the 1919 starters only Luque and Eller remained, and without his shine ball to vex the hitters with, Hod was just about through.

Eppa Rixey (1921–1933), the greatest left-hander the Reds ever had. He was a 25-game winner in 1922.

In Rixey, the Reds obtained a gifted pitcher who was to become one of the most popular personalities in Cincinnati baseball history. Eppa had been with the Phillies since 1912 (he had pitched there for Moran), winning 22 in 1916. In 1920 he had been 11–22 for a last-place club.

At 6 feet, 5 inches Rixey towered on the mound. The Culpeper, Virginia, native was remembered this way by Clyde Sukeforth, who caught for the Reds later in the 1920s:

> He was a fierce competitor and a hard loser. When he pitched, you didn't have to ask who won the game, all you had to do was look at the clubhouse later. If he'd lost, the place would look like a tornado had gone through it. Chairs would be broken up, tables knocked over, equipment thrown around. The ball club didn't like that, needless to say, but what were they going to say to Rixey? That fellow was an institution in Cincinnati.

None of the various realignments helped, as the club dropped to sixth place in 1921. With the lively ball taking off in all directions, the Reds batted .278, but that proved to be the lowest in a league that swatted a lusty .289. Roush reached a career high .352, Groh .331 (after holding out for the first third of the season), Duncan .308, Rube Bressler (converted from pitcher to part-time first baseman–outfielder) .307, and Daubert .306. The .300 hitter had become commonplace.

The lively ball officially came to Redland Field on June 2, 1921, when Duncan hit the first fair ball ever over the left field fence since the erection of that barrier in 1912. (The Reds had only 20 homers in 1921, by far the league's lowest total.)

Cincinnati pitching stood up well in the decline, posting the second best ERA in the league (3.46). Moran's big three were Rixey (19–18), Marquard (17–14) and Luque (17–19). Twenty-year-old right-hander Pete Donohue joined the club that year and was

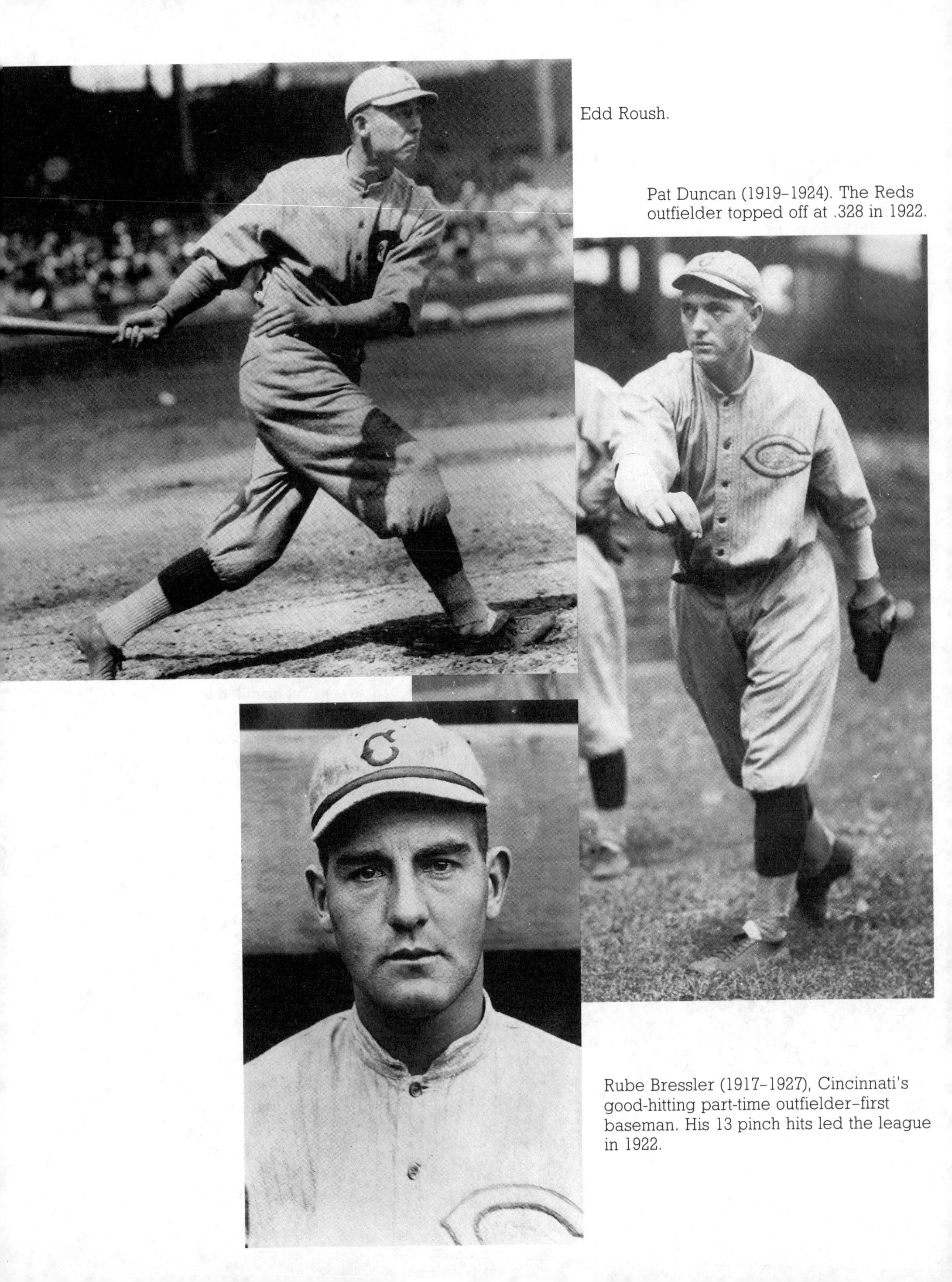

Edd Roush.

Pat Duncan (1919–1924). The Reds outfielder topped off at .328 in 1922.

Rube Bressler (1917–1927), Cincinnati's good-hitting part-time outfielder–first baseman. His 13 pinch hits led the league in 1922.

Cincinnati's three-time twenty-game winner, right-hander Pete Donohue, who worked the Cincinnati mound from 1921 to 1930.

7–6. Donohue had been signed off the campus of Texas Christian University for a $5,000 bonus and brought straight to the big leagues.

If the Reds weren't hitting many home runs, neither were they striking out very often—just 308 times in 1921, which is still the all-time major-league record for fewest whiffs in a season by a team.

Herrmann and Moran went back to the drawing board for the 1922 season, determined to give Cincinnati fans a better product. In December, Groh was traded to the Giants for outfielder George Burns, a speed merchant who was now slightly past his peak, and catcher Mike Gonzalez, who played just one year for the Reds. (In later years Mike, who spoke his own brand of English, filed this memorable scouting report on a young player: "Good field, no hit.")

When the 1922 season opened, the Reds had a new shortstop, Ike Caveney, and a new third baseman, Ralph ("Babe") Pinelli, both obtained from the Pacific Coast League. Pinelli, who had failed in previous trials with the White Sox and Tigers, had a modest 8-year big-league career, but later returned to the National League as an umpire and won lasting fame when he called the final strike of Don Larsen's perfect game in the 1956 World Series.

Also present in the 1922 lineup was outfielder George Harper, acquired from the minors. Not present, however, was Roush. Edd

Outfielder George Burns (1922–1924). His 101 walks led the league in 1924.

Ike Caveney, Cincinnati shortstop from 1922 to 1925.

was stuck fast in another of his holdouts and this time the club was being just as stubborn. It took the summer's heat to soften the concrete on both sides of this particular street; it wasn't until July 23 that the star center fielder showed up to play ball.

Thanks to some sharp hitting—an all-time-high club batting average of .296—the Reds ran a good race in 1922, but finished second to the Giants by 7 games. Roush, sorely missed in the first half, batted .352; Harper, .340; the thirty-eight-year-old Daubert, .336; Duncan, .328; Hargrave, .316; and Pinelli, .305. In addition, utility infielder Lew Fonseca compiled a loud .361 average in 81 games. With 12 home runs, Daubert was the first Redleg to go into double figures in homers since Hoblitzell's 11 in 1911. The club set a franchise record that year with 1,191 singles.

The pitchers again posted the league's second best ERA (3.53), with Rixey the big winner (25–13), followed by young Donohue (18–9), one-year wonder Johnny Couch (16–19) and Luque (13–23).

Moran's club turned in another second-place wrap in 1923, this time finishing just 4½ games behind the Giants. A five-game Giant sweep at Redland Field in early August was a blow from which the Reds never re-

Later a National League umpire, Babe Pinelli was at third base for the Reds from 1922 to 1927. He batted .306 in 1924.

1923 Reds has produced three twenty-game winners in a single season.

Once more Roush led the team at bat, the clockwork-hitting star coming in with a .351 average, followed by Hargrave (.333) and Duncan (.327). Harper, who had done so well the year before, couldn't break into the Roush, Burns, Duncan outfield and batted

George Harper (1922–1924), who batted .340 for the Reds in 1922.

covered. But the club's good showing overall enabled them to set a new home attendance record of 575,063.

While the club's 1923 batting average of .285 was one point lower than the league's mark, the pitching staff recorded the lowest ERA (3.21), thanks mainly to some handsome work by Luque, who had his greatest year with a 27–8 record (most wins in the league) and the lowest ERA, 1.93, which was outstanding in that hit-happy era. The Cuban curveballer also led with 6 shutouts. As an indication of how outstanding Luque was that year, the next best ERA to his was Rixey's 2.80. Eppa was 20–15 and Donohue, 21–15. No National League team since the

Johnny Couch (1922–1923), who gave the Reds a 16–9 year in 1922.

Dolf Luque, a 27-game winner in 1923.

Rube Benton (1910–1915, 1923–1925), who pitched for the Giants in between his stints in Cincinnati.

Carl Mays (1924–1928), always controversial, always a winner.

just .256 in a utility role. Burns, Pinelli, and Caveney were in the .270s, and the veteran Daubert, steady as a spring rain, was a .292 man. Roush led the league with 41 doubles.

Deciding that more pitching was needed, Hermann went out and acquired what sounds like rights to the fifth month of the year—pitchers Carl Mays and Jakie May.

Mays was obtained for cash from the Yankees, for whom he twice had been a twenty-game winner but then worn out his welcome, something the Mays personality was wont to do. The submarine-style right-hander had a 15-year major-league career, compiling an impressive 208–126 record. What Mays is principally remembered for, however, is throwing the pitch that incurred baseball's only on-the-field fatality—the beaning of Cleveland shortstop Ray Chapman at New York's Polo Grounds (at the time home of the Yankees) on August 16, 1920.

If Mays ever felt any remorse over the tragedy, he never showed it (one teammate, in fact, remembered Mays the following spring lecturing young pitchers on the importance of pitching inside). While no one ever questioned his ability on the mound, Mays the man was generally regarded as cold, humorless, devious, and unethical.

Mays's near namesake, Jakie May, was Carl's opposite in every way. A left-hander, the somewhat chubby May had a sunny disposition, a quick smile, and an engaging personality. One Reds player referred to his new

Jakie May (1924–1930) loosening up in spring training in 1925.

Jack Hendricks, who managed the Reds from 1924 through 1929.

That's Hughie Critz (1924–1930) relaxing against a rather ramshackle Cincinnati dugout.

teammates as "Night" and "Day" for the sharp differences in their personalities.

The first thing everyone noticed when the team gathered at their Orlando, Florida, spring camp in 1924 was how drawn and sickly Pat Moran looked. According to one player, Moran looked "as though he'd had the life drained out of him." This inelegant appraisal was brutally unerring. Always a man with good reflexes when a bottle was near, Pat had spent the winter at his Fitchburg, Massachusetts, home drinking more and more heavily, to the point where little else passed between his lips.

When Moran arrived at Orlando he was already a dying man. He had not been off the train very long before he was removed to the hospital, where he died on March 7, at the age of forty-eight. His death was recorded as resulting from Bright's disease.

Herrmann quickly appointed coach Jack Hendricks to succeed Moran. The forty-eight-year-old Hendricks had had brief trials at the turn of the century as an outfielder with the Giants, Cubs, and Senators. A graduate of Northwestern University Law School, he practiced law around Chicago when he wasn't pursuing a baseball career that consisted mainly of minor-league managerial jobs. He managed the Cardinals in 1918 (finishing last) and later managed at Indianapolis. He had just recently signed as a coach with the Reds when Moran died.

Despite some decent hitting (.290) and the league's tightest pitching—the staff again had the lowest ERA (3.12) and issued the fewest walks (293)—the 1924 Reds finished fourth.

Mays baffled National League batters with his submarine deliveries to the tune of a 20–9 record, Donohue was 16–9, Rixey 15–14, and Luque 10–15.

An early-season injury to Fonseca created the need for another second baseman, and the Reds found a good one in Hughie Critz, purchased from the minors. Getting into 102 games, Critz (pronounced as though it began with *cry*) batted .322. Roush kept rolling, batting .348, and leading the league with 21 triples, despite missing 32 games with injuries. Dividing his time between first base and the outfield and getting into 115 games, Rube Bressler batted .347, whereas Pinelli, Hargrave, and outfielder Curt Walker (acquired from the Phillies in May in exchange for Harper) were just over .300.

The reason Bressler was needed at first base was due to injuries and illness suffered by the now forty-year-old Daubert, who got into just 102 games and batted .281. Immediately after the season, Gentleman Jake underwent an operation for appendicitis and gallstones.

Outfielder Curt Walker (1924–1930), a steady hitter. A .318 mark in 1925 was his best.

Cincinnati third baseman and future manager Chuck Dressen, who played for the Reds from 1925 to 1931.

Complications set in and on October 9, 1924, Cincinnati's modest and soft-spoken first baseman died. The season that had begun so ominously for the Reds with Moran's death in the spring, now closed on a similar note of tragedy.

For his 15-year big-league career, the last 6 of which he spent with the Reds, Daubert batted .303, with 10 seasons of more than .300.

The Reds pitching staff led the league in ERA for the third straight year in 1925, logging a 3.38 figure, and for the fourth year in a row walked the fewest batters (324), but the club couldn't do better than third place. The Giants, winners of four straight pennants (the only National League club ever to enjoy such sustained success), were dislodged by a Pittsburgh battering ram that batted a collective .307. (The Pirates were managed by former Cincinnati infielder Bill McKechnie, destined to return and make his place in Reds history.)

Hendricks scratched his head all summer over his first base problem—Daubert had not been replaced. Filling in were newcomers Al Niehaus and Walter Holke, along with Bressler, who also played the outfield. Rube batted .348; Roush, .339; Walker, .338; and Hargrave, .300. The Reds batted .285 as a team in 1925, but in that line-drive era they were outhit by five other teams.

New to the team that year was utility infielder Chuck Dressen. The stocky, always affable, and eternally optimistic Dressen would have a modest playing career, then return later as a long-time big-league manager of five different teams, including the Reds.

The staff produced two top winners in Rixey (21–11) and Donohue (21–14), whereas Luque was 16–18. A back injury sidelined Mays for most of the year, limiting the submariner to a 3–5 record.

To solve their problem at first base, the Reds went out and obtained the man who had suffered baseball's most famous headache. Wally Pipp had been the Yankees' regular first baseman from 1915 until early June 1925. On that June day, Wally reported to Yankee Stadium troubled by a headache. Manager Miller Huggins told him to sit out the day and replaced him with young Lou Gehrig. The rest of that story is engraved in baseball lore.

The thirty-three-year-old Pipp was installed at first base in 1926 and helped the club to a most exciting season. Hendricks's troops gave the Cincinnati fans a stalwart effort and when the last ball had bounced, the Reds were in second place, just two games short of a pennant, finishing with an 87–67 record to 89–65 for the Cardinals.

Backup catcher Val Picinich (1926–1928).

The Reds were in first place through most of June and almost all of July. They fell into third place on August 10, then reversed gears and on September 4 were back on top. After 145 games, the Reds and Cardinals had identical 85–60 records. But at the tail end of a 20-game road trip the Reds stubbed their toes in Boston and Philadelphia and the Cardinals slipped into first place and there remained.

It had been a rousing year at Redland park and Reds fans showed their appreciation by

First baseman Wally Pipp (1926–1929). One day when he was with the Yankees, he had a headache . . .

Outfielder Walter Christenson, whose colorful antics in the outfield earned him the nickname "Cuckoo." He batted .350 in 1926 but a year later was gone.

hitter, an engaging character named Walter Christenson, whose nickname, "Cuckoo," apparently spoke for itself.

"He was a nice fellow," Roush said of Cuckoo, "but he clowned around a lot, like doing somersaults in the outfield during a game. He didn't last too long."

Indeed not. After batting .350 in 114 games in his rookie year, the twenty-seven-year-old Christenson got into fifty-seven games the next year, and that was that for Cuckoo and the big leagues.

Bressler, hitting .357 for 86 games, gave

Clyde Sukeforth (1926–1931), a reserve catcher who batted .354 in 1929.

coming out in sufficient numbers to set a new home attendance record of 672,987.

Disappointed by their club's near miss, the hometown fans could at least cheer the crowning of another Cincinnati batting champion, Bubbles Hargrave taking the crown with a .353 average, the first catcher ever to do so. (In those years, qualifiers for the batting crown needed to play in at least 100 games, which Hargrave barely did—105. Today, a qualifier needs a minimum of 502 plate appearances).

The Reds also had the league's second best

Shortstop Hod Ford (1926–1931) *(left)* and second baseman Hughie Critz.

Right-hander Ray Kolp, who both started and relieved for the Reds from 1927 to 1934.

the club a trio of .350 stickers, while Roush continued his tireless drumbeat at home plate with a .323 mark. The team's .290 average was the league's best, and so were its 120 triples, which remains the Cincinnati club record.

Donohue was 20–14 (tying for most wins); Mays, 19–12; and Rixey, 14–8. For the fifth straight year the staff issued the fewest bases on balls, 324.

The Reds hit just 35 home runs (the pennant-winning Cardinals had the most, 90), but one of them broke a drought. On August 7 at New York's Polo Grounds, Dressen hit the team's first grand-slam home run in fifteen years, since Dick Hoblitzell in 1911.

Immediately after the exciting 1926 season, the Reds slipped into what would prove to be a long anchorage in still waters. This prolonged twilight, which would see them finish in the second division for eleven consecutive years, began with the trade of longtime star Edd Roush. On February 9, 1927, the great center fielder was dealt to the Giants for first baseman George Kelly and a wad of cash of undisclosed amount.

Perhaps Herrmann had simply tired of his star's independent ways or perhaps the boss decided it was time to move his best player while Edd, then thirty-three years old, could still command value. Or maybe Herrmann simply needed that pile of cash. Whatever the reason, after ten outstanding years in Cincinnati, during which he averaged .331, Roush was gone.

Red Lucas (1926–1933), was both a star pitcher and outstanding hitter, leading the league three consecutive times in pinch hits.

The thirty-one-year-old Kelly had been a hard-hitting star on McGraw's four straight pennant winners of the early 1920s, and although he still had some good swings left had seen his best days.

The long decline began for the Reds with a fifth-place finish in 1927. Charles ("Red") Lucas, a right-handed pitcher who could hit, was 18–11 (used frequently as a pinch hitter, the left-handed–hitting Lucas batted .313), followed by Jakie May's 15–12. Rixey and Luque were little better than .500 pitchers, and Donohue slumped to 6–16. The staff once again led in fewest walks with 316. The team had just one .300 bat (Hargrave, .308) and hit the fewest home runs (29).

Failing health ended Garry Herrmann's quarter-century tenure as president of the Reds, the popular executive handing in his resignation on October 15, 1927. Herrmann, who died four years later at the age of seventy-two, was succeeded by Johnson

Reserve outfielder Billy Zitzmann (1919, 1925–1929) was a .297 hitter in 1928, his best year.

McDiarmid, a noted local attorney who had been serving as club secretary.

Hendricks led the 1928 club to another unexciting fifth-place slot. Rixey had his last big year with a 19–18 record, leading the staff. Ethan Allen, a young outfielder playing his second full season, hit .305, highest on

Outfielder Ethan Allen (1926–1930), who batted .305 in 1928.

the team. Kelly supplied a bit of punch, driving in 105 runs, giving the team its first 100-RBI man since Cy Seymour in 1905.

The team that had begun the decade as world champions, closed it out in seventh place, their 66–88 record the club's worst since 1916. The collective batting average of .281 was that year bettered by six other teams in a league that hit .294 overall. Curt Walker's .313 was the best of the Reds.

Despite the team's downhill roll, Lucas managed a 19–12 record. Cincinnati's good-hitting pitcher had a unique distinction in 1929: not only did he lead in complete games (28) but also in pinch hits (13). Donohue, working with an ailing arm the past few seasons, was 10–13 in his last full summer with the Reds. Pete was traded to the Giants the following spring, his big-league career just about over. Luque, with a 5–16 record, was also through in Cincinnati, although the Cuban curveballer would pitch for another six years and do some sharp relief work for the Dodgers and Giants.

For Jack Hendricks, the inevitable came on September 22, the tail end of the 1929 season. Rather than wait for the shove, Jack jumped, on that day handing in his resignation. It was like leaving a slowly flooding ship.

E·I·G·H·T

INTO THE TWILIGHT

AS the country began sinking into economic depression in 1930, major-league batting averages prospered as never before, particularly in the National League. Case in point: the 1930 Cincinnati Reds batted a highly respectable .281 and were outhit by six other clubs, all of whom batted more than .300 (the league as a whole averaged .303 that year). Although the Reds didn't hit as many line shots as their opponents, they did prove more adept than anyone else at picking them up, committing the fewest errors (161), which was about all they had to show for a season that remains the greatest summer-long hitting circus in history.

Under new manager Dan Howley, the Reds finished a soggy seventh with a 59–95 record. A former catcher of little distinction (26 games with the Phillies in 1913), the forty-four-year-old Howley had just completed a three-year turn as skipper of the St. Louis Browns. He was described by a baseball historian as "about the most genial and kindly man who ever managed a big-league team," and a man whose "players swore by him."

Along with a new manager, the Reds also acquired a new owner in businessman Sidney Weil, who had made his packet in real estate and the automobile business. By all accounts, the well-liked Weil was a genuine fan who loved his team and its players but was slightly in the dark when it came to running a ball club.

There were a lot of new faces on the 1930 Reds, two of them quite distinguished of

Dan Howley, who managed the Reds from 1930 through 1932.

Former Detroit Tiger batting star Harry Heilmann (1930, 1932), who gave the Reds a year of solid hitting in 1930.

name. From the Tigers, Weil had purchased Harry Heilmann and from the Yankees, Bob Meusel. Heilmann was one of the great right-handed rappers in history, winner of four batting championships. Meusel was the long-time left fielder on six Yankee pennant winners. Both these stars were past their peaks and played only the one full year with the Reds, although Harry did paste the ball for a .333 average.

Other newcomers were infielders Joe Stripp and Tony Cuccinello and shortstop Leo Durocher, the latter acquired from the Yankees. Leo was, of course, later to become famous as manager of the Brooklyn Dodgers and New York Giants, but in his younger days he was known as a light-hitting, slick-fielding shortstop.

Lucas (14–16) and Benny Frey (11–18) were the only pitchers to win in double figures, with Lucas batting .336 and again leading the league with 14 pinch hits.

In the spring of 1931 the Reds set up at what was to become their long-time training base at Tampa. During this period Weil, who was intrigued by the aura of fading stars, reacquired Edd Roush. After three years with the Giants, Edd had resorted to his old tricks and held out in 1930. The Giants let him sit, and Edd spent the entire summer at his Oakland City, Indiana, farm. New York then decided to wash their hands of him and allow the Reds to deal with their former star.

Joe Stripp (1928–1931), who batted .324 in 1931, then was traded to Brooklyn.

Tony Cuccinello (1930–1931) turned in batting averages of .312 and .315 in his two years with the Reds.

Leo Durocher (1930–1933).

Right-hander Benny Frey (1929–1936), who led the league with 18 losses in 1930. He both started and relieved for the Reds.

Harvey Hendrick (1931–1932) played first base for the Reds in 1931 and batted .315.

Howley's club landed in last place in 1931 despite .300 years from first baseman Harvey Hendrick (acquired from Brooklyn), Stripp, and Cuccinello. Lucas (14–13) was the only man on the staff to log a winning record. Right-hander Silas Johnson led the league in losses (11–19). Not a bad pitcher at all, Silas was doomed to labor for some of the worst teams in Cincinnati history. Working for the Reds until 1935, he compiled a record with the team of 46–86.

Roush retired for keeps in January 1932, and two months later Weil swung a sizable deal with the Dodgers. In exchange for infielders Stripp and Cuccinello and catcher Clyde Sukeforth, the Reds obtained catcher Ernie Lombardi, outfielder Babe Herman, and third baseman Wally Gilbert.

The colorful Herman, a one-time .393 hitter for the Dodgers, and Gilbert each played just the one season for the Reds, but Lombardi went on to become a Cincinnati legend.

Known equally for his ferocious line drives—it was said that no one ever hit a ball harder—and his slowness afoot, so slow he looked like he was running through waist-high water, Ernie had played one year for the Dodgers. Preferring to keep catcher Al Lopez, Brooklyn had dealt Big Ernie to the Reds.

Lombardi's slow-motion pace along the baselines enabled the left side of opposing infields to play him as far back as the edge of the outfield grass, where they found protection from his bullet shots, and from where they were frequently able to throw him out at first base. Nevertheless, Ernie (sometimes known as "Schnozz" for his door-knocker-size nose) was a steady .300 hitter.

Another spring deal brought Cardinal outfielder Chick Hafey to the Reds in exchange for Benny Frey, Hendrick, and cash. Hafey was one of the league's top stars. Only twenty-nine years old, Chick had annoyed his employers with demands for more money (to an extremely tight-fisted St. Louis ownership, Hafey's demands might be described as a cardinal sin). In addition, Chick was suffering

Larry Benton (1930–1934), who pitched some pretty good ball for some pretty bad Cincinnati teams.

A good pitcher laboring for inept teams, Silas Johnson (1928–1936) led the league with 19 losses in 1931 and 22 in 1934.

Ernie Lombardi (1932–1941). They weren't kidding when they said he had big hands.

increasingly from sinus trouble, which darkened his future, despite his having won the batting crown with a .349 average in 1931. Trading a reigning batting titlist was unusual indeed, but the Cardinals had slugging young Joe Medwick about to be graduated from their farm system. (Within two months, the Cardinals returned both Hendrick and Frey to the Reds in cash transactions.)

Illness limited Hafey to 83 games, in which he batted .344. But even a full season from Chick would not have made much difference. Herman batted .326 and led the league with 19 triples, and Lombardi was a .303 hitter. Lucas (13–15) and Johnson (13–17) led the staff.

After a second straight last-place finish in 1932, Howley was gone and Donie Bush was in. A long-time shortstop for the Detroit Tigers during the heyday of Ty Cobb, Bush had previously managed Washington, Pittsburgh (winning the pennant in 1927), and the Chicago White Sox.

Soon after Bush was hired, in November 1932, Sidney Weil, beginning to feel a cash pinch that would soon force him out of baseball, sold Babe Herman to the Cubs for

Babe Herman (1932, 1935–1936) hit .326 for the Reds in 1932.

$80,000 and four players, none of whom were of much help to the Reds. In December, the club obtained veteran first baseman Sunny Jim Bottomley from the Cardinals. One of the league's most feared hitters during his long Cardinal career, the then thirty-two-year-old Bottomley had begun to slide.

On May 7, 1933, the Reds made another deal with the Cardinals, one that was to pay large dividends for the Reds in the future. To St. Louis went Durocher and pitchers Dutch Henry and Jack Ogden for infielder Sparky Adams and pitchers Allyn Stout and Paul Derringer. While Durocher helped solidify the Cardinal infield and was part of the "Gashouse Gang" world champions of 1934, the

Chick Hafey (1932–1935, 1937), one of the great ball players of the time. His career was impeded and finally aborted by injuries.

Outfielder Taylor Douthit (1931–1933), who came to the Reds after some fine years with the Cardinals.

Sidney Weil *(right)* and manager Donie Bush at the Reds' spring training camp at Tampa in March 1933. Weil apparently felt that working out with his team was one of the prerogatives of ownership.

big, high-kicking, right-handed Derringer was to go on to become one of the great pitchers in Cincinnati history.

But Derringer and the rest of the Reds suffered through a wretched 1933 season, which saw the club take eighth-place lumps for the third year in a row. The club batting average of .246 was the league's lowest since the dead-ball days of 1918. This sluggish attack victimized Derringer in particular, who, despite a respectable 3.23 ERA, was forced to endure a horrendous 7–27 season (two of the losses incurred with the Cardinals). Hafey's .304 average led the team.

The season marked the end of the long career of Eppa Rixey, who had been pitching less and less each year. The forty-two-year-old left-hander went out a winner with a 6–3 record, rounding out a lifetime ledger of 266–251.

Soon after the close of the 1933 season, a near bankrupt Sidney Weil resigned as Reds president and turned the club over to the

Paul Derringer (1933–1942), one of the greatest of all Cincinnati pitchers.

Infielder Tony Piet (1934–1935).

Central Trust Company. Needing someone to run the franchise, the bank appointed Leland Stanford ("Larry") MacPhail.

Fiery, tempestuous, outrageous, and innovative, MacPhail was precisely the man any moribund franchise needed. Originally a lawyer, with a degree from George Washington University, McPhail saw service in World War I (his escapades in that adventure included a harebrained, nearly successful attempt to kidnap Germany's kaiser). After the war he drifted into baseball as president of the Columbus, Ohio, team of the American Association, a Cardinal outlet. After four years with Columbus, MacPhail had a dispute with the Cardinals and was canned. It was at this point that he was handed the task of resuscitating the Cincinnati Reds.

MacPhail, who a writer was to describe as "Hurricane Larry" when the aggressive, nonstop redhead was building a Brooklyn Dodgers pennant winner in the early 1940s, went immediately to work.

The winds of change quickly blew Donie Bush out of the managerial chair, and in late December MacPhail, ever the showman, tried to buy the aging Babe Ruth from the Yankees, with the intention of making Babe the player-manager. The Yankees, however, said no.

One of MacPhail's first deals was to trade Lucas to Pittsburgh for outfielder Adam Comorosky and infielder Tony Piet. In January 1934, Larry obtained long-time catcher Bob O'Farrell from the Cardinals and appointed him manager. (O'Farrell's playing career was just about at an end.)

It was in February 1934, however, that MacPhail scored his greatest coup. Imagina-

Southpaw Tony Freitas (1934–1936), who both started and relieved for the Reds.

Left to right: Larry MacPhail, manager Chuck Dressen, and Powel Crosley. Dressen, who managed the Reds from 1934 to 1937, is posing with his bosses in the spring of 1935.

tion, determination, and aggressiveness could carry a team only so far; what was needed to oil these dynamos of the spirit was money. With the bank's blessings, Larry set out to find someone with the money to buy the team and the faith to back up Larry's bold ventures. The man the persuasive MacPhail met and convinced to do just these things was Powel Crosley, Jr.

Crosley was a modest, likeable man who had made his fortune as an inventor and manufacturer of automobiles, refrigerators, and radios. When MacPhail told Crosley that there was a chance of the nearly lifeless Cincinnati franchise being moved to another city, the sentimental millionaire agreed to the purchase.

"Cincinnati is the birthplace of professional baseball," Crosley said. "I cannot imagine this city not being represented in the major leagues."

So in February 1934 Powel Crosley took over the team, promising MacPhail there would be money with which to rebuild. In tribute to the new owner, the flamboyant MacPhail changed the name of the team's home park from Redland Field to Crosley Field, a name that remained unchanged as long as the park stood.

Despite all the hectic front-office activity that saw players coming and going all season, the Reds were doomed to another year in the dust bin, this time with a 52–99 record and .344 percentage, the worst in club history. Attendance dwindled to little more than 200,000.

For the 1934 Reds the high point, in a sense, came on June 8, when MacPhail flew the team from Cincinnati to Chicago in two

Outfielder Johnny Moore (1933–1934), who was a lifetime .300 hitter.

The exterior of Crosley Field in the mid-1930s.

American Airlines cabin planes, making the Reds the first big-league team to travel from one city to another by air. (One coach and seven players, unwilling to face this brave new world, took the overnight sleeper to Chicago.)

With the team dawdling along at a 26–58 record in late July, the impatient MacPhail fired O'Farrell and replaced him with the club's one-time third baseman, Chuck Dressen. The ebullient thirty-five-year-old Dressen had ended his playing career the year before and was managing at Nashville when Larry summoned him back to the big leagues.

Although the team played slightly better under their new skipper, there was no way that last place could be avoided, and there the club snuggled at the end of the season, 42 games distant from the top, the third largest deficit in Reds history.

Derringer got through the debacle with a 15–21 record, Lombardi batted .305, and at season's end the club brought young first baseman Frank McCormick up for quick inspection. In twelve games he batted .313. Little suspected at the time, some puffs of breath were being breathed into the corpse that was the Cincinnati Reds.

N•I•N•E

LIGHTING THE WAY

ON May 24, 1935, the city that had introduced professional baseball to America was the scene of a landmark event in the game's evolution.

Larry MacPhail had long believed that night baseball was desirable, inevitable, and necessary. He had introduced after-dark baseball at Columbus and it had been successful. The major leagues, however, were another story. As far as most club owners were concerned, their game was absolutely perfect and could not be improved on. Any new idea smacked of sedition. Clark Griffith, one of the bulwarks of the conservative old game, had this to say of night ball:

> There is no chance of night baseball ever becoming popular in the bigger cities. . . . High-class baseball cannot be played at night under artificial light. Furthermore, the benefits derived from attending the game are largely due to fresh air and sunshine. Night air and electric lights are a poor substitute.

But history shows that the Larry MacPhails have consistently triumphed over the Clark Griffiths. Calling on all of his powers of persuasion, Larry talked the baseball hierarchy into allowing seven night games at Crosley Field in 1935. Many people both in and out of baseball described Larry's adventure as "an experiment" or "a fad." MacPhail, who would later bring arc lights to Brooklyn's Ebbets Field and to New York's Yankee Stadium (when he was part-owner of the Yankees in the immediate postwar years), knew better.

Big-league baseball's first night game was scheduled for May 23, 1935, but was postponed for twenty-four hours by rain. And so it was played on May 24. The event was duly noted in the White House, where at 8:30 P.M.

Crosley Field on the night of May 24, 1935. The crowd is watching big-league baseball's first night game.

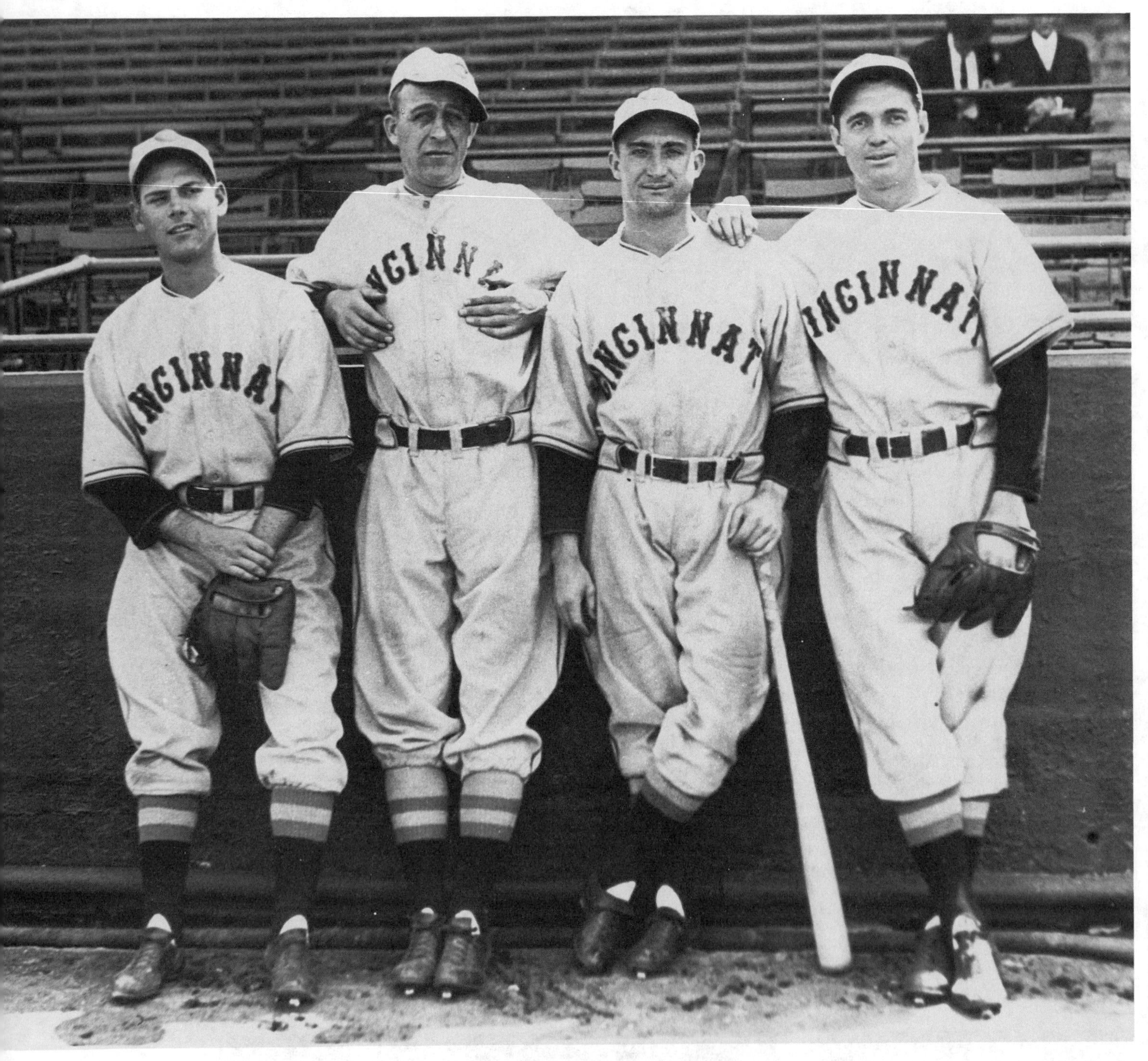

Cincinnati's 1935 infield *(left to right):* second baseman Alex Kampouris (1934–1938), first baseman Jim Bottomley (1933–1935), shortstop Billy Myers (1935–1940), and third baseman Lew Riggs (1935–1940).

President Franklin Delano Roosevelt pressed a button that magically lit the 632 lamps that suddenly rolled back the night over a green-grassed patch of Ohio and sent baseball into its new era.

A crowd of 20,422—sizable for a last-place team in the Depression years—bore witness as Paul Derringer beat the Phillies, 2–1. And all of those club owners who had sighed and decided to humor MacPhail couldn't help but raise their eyebrows at those attendance figures.

Al Hollingsworth (1935–1938), one of Cincinnati's better starters in the mid-1930s.

Second-string catcher Gilly Campbell (1935–1937) showing the photographer how it's done.

Right-hander Don Brennan (1934–1937), who worked primarily in relief for the Reds.

But by day or by night, the Reds were still a second-division team, although obviously improving. Dressen brought his club home sixth in 1935, which, after four straight summers in the cellar was something of an achievement. (Between the arc lights and some spirited play, attendance jumped from 206,773 in 1934 to 448,247 a year later).

When Hafey left the team early in the 1935 season because of an injury, MacPhail reacquired Babe Herman, who got into 92 game^ for the Reds and leveled league pitching for .335 average. Lombardi swung the club' other thundering bat, coming in with a career-high .343 mark, striking out just six times in 332 official at bats, a remarkable statistic for a man who took his full rip at home plate. The lineup also began to radiate with young talent, particularly shortstop Billy Myers, third baseman Lew Riggs, and outfielder Ival Goodman, the latter leading in triples with 18. The outline of the 1939–1940 pennant winners was now becoming clearer.

The pitching was all Derringer. The big right-hander was 22–13 and the only man on the staff to win in double figures.

In 1936 the Reds finished fifth, the first time since 1928 that they had done as well. Just as this relative success was being re-

Kiki Cuyler (1935–1937). This one-time great outfielder for the Pirates and Cubs played his twilight years for the Reds, batting .326 in 1936.

Warren Giles *(left)* and Powel Crosley.

corded, MacPhail, on September 18, resigned. Always impatient, always impulsive, Larry was not one to stay in one place for very long. Satisfied that he had succeeded in turning the team around, MacPhail departed, soon to resurface as general manager of the Dodgers.

MacPhail's successor was Warren Giles, about to begin one of major-league baseball's most distinguished executive careers. Giles had already enjoyed considerable success working in the Cardinal farm system when Powel Crosley tapped him for the job in Cincinnati. The amiable, baseball-wise Giles was to remain in the Reds front office until 1952, when he was elected president of the National League, a job he filled until 1970.

The modest success of 1936 must have seemed like a mirage to Cincinnati fans a year later when the team went into jarring reverse and finished last again. Lombardi was the only Redleg to pound the ball with authority, racking up a .334 average, while free-spirited left-hander Lee Grissom was the biggest winner with a 12–17 record. (On January 27, 1937, when the Ohio River stormed over its banks and brought Cincinnati the worst flood in the city's history, Grissom and a friend rowed a boat across the center field fence and posed for what became a famous picture—the two men becalmed in a rowboat in twenty-one feet of water in the midst of Crosley Field.)

A new general manager usually means a new field manager, so when Giles took over, Dressen's days were numbered, with the

Lee Grissom, a colorful character with a red-hot fastball. A sore arm curtailed him early. He pitched for the Reds from 1934 to 1939, leading the league in shutouts in 1937.

That's Lee Grissom (waving hat) and companion becalmed in a rowboat in the midst of Crosley Field during the Ohio River flood of 1937. Note the height of the water in the lower grandstands.

number being reduced by the team's mediocre play. Dressen was fired on September 13, at which point coach Bobby Wallace took over for the rest of the season.

On October 9, 1937, Giles announced the signing of Cincinnati's new manager—Bill McKechnie. The infielder who had first come to the Reds in 1916 as part of the Christy Mathewson trade had now made it all the way back. After a modest playing career spent in the gray regions of a .250 batting average, McKechnie had enjoyed some success as a manager, winning pennants in Pittsburgh (1925) and St. Louis (1928). For the previous eight years he had been managing the Boston Braves, doing as well with that weak team as any man could have.

A deeply devout man, patient and empathetic, McKechnie exuded an aura of dignity that had won the respectfully given nickname "Deacon Bill." A shrewd evaluator not only of talent but of personality, McKechnie seemed to have an innate understanding of the psyche of each of his players, enabling him to maintain a harmony rare for a team of twenty-five highly competitive athletes.

The 1938 season put the Reds at the very threshold of success. It was a year that saw a winning team coming together and that also saw one of baseball's most sublime individual achievements, one that has remained in glittering solitude in the annals of the game. The season also saw the Reds make one of the most successful trades in their history.

In a pennant race that had four teams crowding the top, the Reds finished fourth, just six games behind the pennant-winning Cubs. It was the club's most successful season since their second-place finish in 1926 and their appreciative fans showed up in record numbers, setting a new franchise attendance mark of 706,756.

Frank McCormick, now ripened on the vine, took over first base, and if there had been a Rookie of the Year award in 1938, it probably would have gone to Frank, who

Bill McKechnie, Cincinnati's highly respected manager from 1938 through 1946.

Right-hander Gene Schott (1935–1938), who won 11 games in 1936, second best on the staff.

broke in with a .327 average and a league-leading 209 hits. Second baseman Lonny Frey (acquired from the Cubs), shortstop Billy Myers and third baseman Lew Riggs teamed with McCormick to give the club a strong infield. The team now had defensive whiz Harry Craft in center, while right-fielder Ival Goodman clubbed 30 home runs to set a new all-time Cincinnati record.

For Ernie Lombardi, 1938 was a memorable year. The big catcher enhanced his great popularity by hitting .342 and winning the batting crown, only the second catcher in major-league history (Bubbles Hargrave had been the first) to earn the distinction. Ernie's year was capped in the fall with the National League's Most Valuable Player award, the first Reds player to be so honored since the award was instituted in 1931 by the Baseball Writers Association of America.

Paul Derringer came back after two so-so seasons to deliver a 21–14 record. But the most talked-about pitcher in baseball that year was Cincinnati's hitherto little-known left-hander Johnny Vander Meer.

Vander Meer had joined the team in 1937 and worked to a 3–5 record, creating two indelible impressions: he was breathtakingly

The estimable Frank McCormick (1934, 1937–1945), who led the league in hits in his first three full years.

Lonny Frey (1938–1943, 1946), second baseman on the 1939–1940 pennant winners. His 22 steals led the league in 1940.

fast and frighteningly wild. Under McKechnie's patient handling, however, Johnny found at least the general location of home plate and in 1938 he was inserted into the rotation.

On June 11, 1938, Vander Meer entertained the Crosley Field crowd by victimizing Casey Stengel's Boston team with the first no-hitter delivered by a Reds pitcher since Hod Eller's in 1919.

Four days later, on June 15, Johnny took the mound again. Even before the first pitch was thrown, the game was already a celebrated event—the first night game in Ebbets Field history. With Dodger GM Larry MacPhail orchestrating the show, there were marching bands, speeches, track-and-field events, and other promotional schemes to highlight the historic night. It was Vander Meer who made it truly historic.

Vander Meer was blazing fast that night; he didn't start throwing his curve with any consistency until the seventh inning. After eight innings he still had not allowed a hit. Going into the bottom of the ninth, the Cincinnati southpaw was on the brink of an unprecedented achievement, and even the normally vigorously partisan Dodger fans were cheering him on (the Reds were comfortably ahead, 6–0).

After retiring the first man to face him in the bottom of the ninth, Vander Meer, by his

(BELOW) Harry Craft (1937–1942), one of the best defensive center fielders of his day.

(ABOVE) Shortstop Billy Myers.

Outfielder Ival Goodman (1935–1942) gave the Reds some solid hitting, peaking at .323 in 1939.

Lew Riggs, who lost his third base job to Billy Werber in 1939.

Johnny Vander Meer at work on the Ebbets Field mound on the night of June 15, 1938, on the way to his second straight no-hitter.

own admission "pressing a little," walked the bases loaded. A visit from McKechnie settled him down. He retired the next man on a force at home, and now, one out away from a second consecutive no-hitter, faced former Reds shortstop Leo Durocher. Vander Meer remembered it vividly:

> I got two strikes on him and then something happened that I'll never forget as long as I live. The umpire was Bill Stewart, and incidentally, he was a good one. But Stewart was kind of short and occasionally had trouble seeing over big Lombardi. Well, I hit that outside corner with about two inches to spare, and he missed it. He called it a ball. Lombardi gave him a little blast, but I didn't say anything. There was no sense in upsetting myself, not in that spot.
>
> On the next pitch Durocher lifted an easy fly ball to Harry Craft in center field, and that was it. And do you know who was the first guy out to the mound? Bill Stewart. He came running out and he said, "John, I blew that pitch. If you hadn't got him out I was the guy to blame for it." That was real nice of Bill to say that; but I'm just wondering: If Durocher had got a base hit, would he have come out and said it anyway?

In his next start, against Boston, Vander Meer opened with three more hitless innings until Debs Garms broke the spell with a single through the box. Vander Meer's 21 consecutive hitless innings remains the National League record.

In the midst of Vander Meer's magic, on

Left to right: Bill McKechnie, Johnny Vander Meer, and Ernie Lombardi.

June 13, 1938, the Reds engineered their critical trade. From the Philadelphia Phillies they obtained right-hander Bucky Walters, in exchange for catcher Spud Davis, left-hander Al Hollingsworth, and $50,000.

Walters had originally come to the major leagues in 1931 as a third baseman with the Boston Braves. He later played for the Boston Red Sox before being sold to the Phillies in June 1934.

"He always had a live arm," one of his Red Sox teammates recalled years later. "His pegs to first base sometimes had so much on them the first baseman couldn't handle them. But nobody thought then of making him a pitcher."

Nor did Walters want to pitch. But when Bucky got to Philadelphia, manager Jimmie Wilson was more impressed with his arm than with his .250 bat. He finally induced Walters to "pitch a few innings" at the end of the 1934 season. A year later Bucky was in the rotation, firing his hard, sinking fastball and doing quite well for a wretched Phillies club. Then, in June 1938, the Phillies, perenially cash hungry in those days, dispatched him to the Reds. Bucky went 11–6 for Cincinnati over the remainder of the season. Along with Derringer and Vander Meer (15–10), the club now had the strongest pitching to show at Crosley Field in more than a decade. (Injuries had sidelined Grissom for much of the year.)

In 1939, the Cubs, winners of three pennants in seven years, were fading, while the

Dodgers and Cardinals, who would soon be waging ferocious battles for the pennant, were not quite ready. There was, in a sense, a temporary power vacuum in the National League, and Bill McKechnie and his Cincinnati Reds stepped in and effectively filled it.

On March 16, 1939, the Reds inserted the final piece into their puzzle with the purchase from the Philadelphia Athletics of third baseman Billy Werber. The hustling Werber, a 7-year American League veteran, proved to be exactly the man the Reds needed. His arrival made a utility man of Lew Riggs. The McCormick, Frey, Myers, Werber combine was one of the best infields in Reds history. In the outfield the club had Craft, Goodman, veteran Wally Berger, Lee Gamble, and a man with the resounding name of Nino Bongiovanni. Behind the plate was Lombardi, backed up by a young catcher from the Yankee farm system, Willard Hershberger, destined a year later to become one of baseball's saddest headlines.

Bill McKechnie *(right)* greeting a new acquisition, Bucky Walters, in June 1938. Walters (1938–1948) became one of the greatest pitchers in Cincinnati history.

One of the greatest of all hitters during his long career in the American League, outfielder Al Simmons was with the Reds briefly in 1939.

The pitching was led by Walters and Derringer, one of the great mound duos in baseball history, followed by right-handers Whitey Moore and Gene ("Junior") Thompson. Arm miseries were to handicap Vander Meer throughout most of the year.

Wally Berger, one-time slugging outfielder of the Boston Braves, was with the Reds from 1938–1940. He batted .307 for the Reds in 1938.

The Reds began signaling their intentions in May, running off a 12-game winning streak—still the club record—and when it ended on May 27 the team was in first place. And there they remained for the rest of the season, fighting off the spirited pursuit of the St. Louis Cardinals. The matter was settled in head-to-head combat at the end of September. With the Reds up by $3^1/_2$ games, the Cardinals came to town for a 4-game matchup. Thompson won the opener, but then the Cardinals beat Grissom and Walters, narrowing the lead to $2^1/_2$. The following day, however, Derringer trimmed the Cardinals, 5–3, and the first Cincinnati pennant in twenty years was ready to fly.

The most conspicuous contributors to Cincinnati's 97–57 pennant-winning record were Walters and Derringer. Bucky, who was later voted the league's MVP (the Cy Young award was not established until 1956), was 27–11, leading in wins, complete games (31), innings (319), strikeouts (137), and ERA (2.29).

Third baseman Billy Werber (1939–1941) led the league in runs in 1939.

That's Frank McCormick scoring an artful run. The other men in the picture are not identified.

Reserve outfielder Nino Bongiovanni (1938–1939).

Ernie Lombardi.

Bucky Walters, the earned run average leader in 1939 and 1940.

Derringer, not far behind his teammate in every category, was 25–7. Always noted for his control, "Oom Paul" walked just 35 men in 301 innings. Supplementing the 52 wins registered by the Big Two, were Moore (13–12) and Thompson (13–5).

In his second full year, McCormick again led in hits (209) and also in RBIs (128, a new club record), while batting .332. Goodman was at .323; Frey, .291; Werber, .289; and Lombardi, .287. The Cardinals outhit the Reds, .294 to .278, and outscored them, 779 to 767, but Cincinnati had Bucky and Paul, and that was the difference.

(A changing world note: on August 26 that

Paul Derringer in a classic pose.

Paul Derringer *(left)* and Bucky Walters, who won 52 games for the Reds in 1939.

year the Reds and Dodgers participated in the first-ever televised big-league game, a double-header played at Brooklyn's Ebbets Field. Home telecasts from Crosley Field began in 1948).

Years later, when asked about the 1939 World Series, Frank McCormick smiled wryly and said, "What World Series?"

It was Cincinnati's misfortune that October to run into a great team at the pinnacle of success. Joe McCarthy's Yankee jugger-

Whitey Moore (1936–1942), starting and relieving, won 13 for the 1939 pennant winners.

That's Ival Goodman striking out in the first inning of the 1939 World Series opener between the Reds and Yankees. The catcher is Bill Dickey, the umpire Bill McGowan.

naut had just won its fourth straight pennant and had already taken three straight World Series.

This was the Yankee team that had lost Lou Gehrig in the spring and still won by 17 games. It was the team of Joe DiMaggio, rookie slugger Charlie Keller, Tommy Henrich, Bill Dickey, Joe Gordon, Red Rolfe, George Selkirk, with a pitching staff that featured Lefty Gomez, Red Ruffing, Monte Pearson, and ace reliever Johnny Murphy.

The Reds were in it only in Games 1 and 4. The opener, at Yankee Stadium, saw Derringer lose a 2–1 heartbreaker to Ruffing, New York winning in the bottom of the ninth on a Keller triple and Dickey single.

Game 2 belonged to Pearson, who no-hit the Reds until Lombardi singled in the eighth, and concluded with a two-hitter, 4–0, beating Walters.

When the Series moved to Cincinnati, the Yankee power tore loose. Although they collected just five hits off of Thompson, four of them were home runs—two by Keller, and one each by DiMaggio and Dickey. The Yankees won it, 7-3.

Trying to stave off the humiliation of a sweep, the Reds sent Derringer back to the mound in Game 4. The game was scoreless until the top of the seventh, when Keller and Dickey homered, giving the Yankees a 2–0 lead. But the Reds went ahead with three in the deep end of the seventh, scored another in the eighth and, with Walters on the mound now, took a 4–2 lead into the top of the ninth. Bucky was unable to nail it down, the Yankees scoring two to tie.

Then came a nightmarish—for Reds fans—top of the tenth. Frank Crosetti opened with a walk, was sacrificed to second, and went to third when Myers booted Keller's grounder. Then occurred the play by which an otherwise routine Series has come to be remembered.

DiMaggio rifled a single to right, scoring Crosetti, and when Goodman misplayed the ball, Keller also headed for the plate. As he scored, the burly Keller barreled into Lombardi, knocking the big catcher momentarily senseless, with the ball lying nearby. Seeing this, DiMaggio headed for the plate and scored without a play being made on him.

The image of the big Lombardi lying on the ground, the ball a few feet away, with DiMaggio scoring, gave the writers the Series handle that had thus far been missing: "Lombardi's snooze." It was eminently unfair to Ernie, who had been dazed in the collision with Keller.

"It was the big story of the Series," Walters said later, "and it was a big story about nothing. The damaging runs had already scored."

The final score was 7–4.

Behind strong pitching, a tight defense, and timely hitting, the Reds repeated as National League champions in 1940. With one excep-

The celebrated "Lombardi snooze" in the top of the tenth inning of Game 4 of the 1939 World Series. Joe DiMaggio has just slid home safely. Bucky Walters is at the right and the umpire is ex-Cincinnati third baseman Babe Pinelli, who looks as though he is counting to "ten" over the dazed Lombardi.

Mike McCormick (1940–1943, 1946) batted .300 in his rookie year.

tion, McKechnie's starting lineup was the same as the year before. The new man was outfielder Mike McCormick (no relation to Frank), who broke in with a .300 batting average.

The National League had been the home of tight pennant races for nearly a decade, the largest margin since 1931 being five games. The 1940 Reds, however, broke the pattern, winning by a comfortable 12-game spread, ending with a 100–53 record, at the time the most wins ever by a Cincinnati club. The Reds made the league's fewest errors (117, a new major-league record low), and the staff logged the best ERA (3.05). This manner of tight play enabled the club to go 41–17 in 1-run games.

The strong pitching of Walters and Derringer was abetted by Junior Thompson and two newcomers acquired via trades, right-handers Jim Turner and Joe Beggs. Turner was the fourth starter, and Beggs was the club's bullpen ace.

After fighting off the Dodgers over the season's first half, the Reds took over first place for keeps on July 7 and from then on began a smooth journey to the end of the season.

Right-hander Gene (''Junior'') Thompson, (1939–1942), who both started and relieved for the Reds. He was 16–9 in 1940.

There was, however, a shattering event that marred the club's summer of satisfaction. On August 3, the club's backup catcher, Willard Hershberger, committed suicide by cutting his throat with a razor blade in his room in a Boston hotel.

Well liked by his teammates, the thirty-year-old catcher was also recalled as "quiet," "moody," "occasionally depressed." During the days leading up to his suicide, Hershberger seemed deeply troubled. Noticing this, McKechnie had had dinner with him the night before the tragedy, during which Hershberger had apparently unburdened himself to the skipper.

As McKechnie and Hershberger were crossing the hotel lobby heading for the dining room, Frank McCormick remembered, "Willard obviously was in some emotional distress; his eyes were all welled up with tears."

Willard Hershberger (1938–1940). The mystery was never solved.

Relief ace Joe Beggs (1940–1944, 1946–1947). He was 12–3 in 1940.

McKechnie seemed satisfied that he had succeeded in settling Hershberger's troubled spirit, but when the catcher did not show up at the ballpark the next day, a concerned McKechnie sent someone back to the hotel, where the body was discovered. Whatever brought Willard Hershberger to his lonely and poignant end was never discovered, though according to McCormick, McKechnie knew what it was.

" 'I know what the story is,' " McCormick said McKechnie told him. " 'I know what

Ival Goodman.

Frank McCormick.

Outfielder Jimmy Ripple (1940–1941), one of the Reds' hitting stars in the 1940 World Series.

happened, but I'm going to my grave with it.' And he did. Whatever it was that Willard confided in him, McKechnie would never tell it. That's the kind of man he was."

In his third year as Lombardi's backup, Hershberger (who had batted .345 in 63 games in 1939) was hitting .309 at the time of his death.

McKechnie called a team meeting on the day following the tragedy. McCormick recalled:

> He knew we were down. It was pretty somber. Bill told us to be kind to Willard's memory, and that nobody on the team was responsible in the slightest way for what had happened. Then he wound up the meeting by saying, "And we're giving Willard's World Series share to his mother." That jolted us back to life. That was McKechnie's way of saying there was still a lot of baseball to be played and that we were going to win. Bill McKechnie was quite a leader, wasn't he?

The Reds clinched their second straight pennant in Philadephia on September 18, 1940, beating the Phillies 4–3 in thirteen innings.

Although not as overwhelming as the previous year, Walters (22–10) and Derringer (20–12) were still the league's best tandem. Thompson was 16–9; Turner, 14–7; and Beggs, 12–3 coming out of the bullpen. For the second year in a row Walters was the ERA leader (2.48).

Lombardi's .319 topped the team, and for the third straight year Frank McCormick led in hits (191), tying a record. The star first baseman also led with 44 doubles and was voted the league's MVP, making it three Reds in a row so honored. McCormick's 127 RBIs were one under his own club record. Frey, Myers, and Werber were the rest of the infield, with Eddie Joost sharing some time at shortstop with Myers. Goodman, Craft, and Mike McCormick were the outfield, with late-season help from Jimmy Ripple, who was acquired from the Dodgers and batted .307 in thirty-two games.

Just before the opening of the World Series, the Reds suffered a couple of injuries that seriously diminished their October chances. First, Lombardi was sidelined with an ankle injury, and then Frey broke a toe in a dugout accident. Thus the Reds headed into the Series all but deprived of their catcher and second baseman, each of whom could do little more than pinch-hit.

The Reds had Joost to fill in at second for Frey, but catching was a serious problem. With Hershberger gone and Lombardi hurting, the team was strapped. Into the breach stepped coach Jimmie Wilson (the same Wilson who as manager of the Phillies had converted Walters to pitching). Formerly a top receiver with the Phillies and Cardinals, Jimmie had just about hung up his shin guards, having played in a handful of games for the Reds in 1940. But the emergency bell had rung, and Wilson was the man McKechnie sent out in response.

Opposing the Reds in the Series were Del Baker's Detroit Tigers, who had finally, after a close-run race, derailed the Yankee express. The Tigers had two of baseball's all-time greats in outfielder Hank Greenberg and second baseman Charlie Gehringer, a slugging first baseman in Rudy York and some splendid players in outfielders Barney McCosky and Bruce Campbell, third baseman Pinky Higgins, shortstop Dick Bartell, and catcher Birdie Tebbetts. The club's ace was the colorful, rubber-armed, right-hander Bobo Newsom, backed up by righties Schoolboy Rowe and Tommy Bridges. (With twenty-year-old right-hander Fred Hutchinson also on the squad, the Tigers had, along with Tebbetts, two future Cincinnati managers.)

Jimmie Wilson (1939–1940), the veteran catcher who made a notable "comeback" in the 1940 World Series.

The Series opened in Cincinnati with a 7–2 Tiger victory, as Detroit disposed of Derringer with a 5-run second and then followed Newsom all the way home. But Walters restored the balance the next day with a 3-hit, 5–3 win over Rowe.

Game 3, in Detroit, was won by Bridges and the Tigers, 7–4, with Turner the loser. Derringer evened it up in Game 4 with a 5–2 win over young right-hander Dizzy Trout. But then in the pivotal Game 5, the Tigers hammered away hard and early at Thompson, and Newsom cruised to 3-hit, 8–0 shutout.

Down three games to two with the Series moving back to Cincinnati, Reds fans were dejected. But Bill McKechnie was upbeat, telling Giles, "There are two games left and we've got Walters and Derringer."

The skipper's faith was not misplaced. Bucky came through handsomely, firing a 5-hit, 4–0 shutout to beat Rowe. The former third baseman crowned the most crucial victory of his career with an eighth-inning home run.

"I was on air going around the bases," he said. "I don't think my feet touched the ground once."

Game 7 found Baker strapped for a pitcher, and the Tiger skipper turned to his ace, the ever-ready, remorselessly self-confident Newsom, who would come back on just one day's rest. Derringer would be working on two day's rest.

Despite their short recovery time, the two lion-hearted aces grappled tenaciously in an epic duel. Detroit scored in the top of the third and Bobo guarded the precious run through inning after tense inning. Then, in the Cincinnati seventh, Frank McCormick led off with a double. Jimmy Ripple, one of the hitting stars of the Series, followed with another double, the ball falling just beyond Campbell's reach in right field. McCormick, having had to wait to see if the ball would be caught, got a late start. Rounding third, he hesitated as the relay came to shortstop Bartell, who assumed McCormick was scoring easily. Gehringer shouted to Bartell to go home with the ball, but because of the roar of the Cincinnati crowd, Bartell did not hear him. McCormick then went into high gear and scored the tying run.

Jimmie Wilson then sacrificed Ripple to third, from where he scored on Myers's fly to deep center. Derringer held the narrow margin through the next two innings and Cincin-

Detroit's Bobo Newsom and Paul Derringer extending a less than enthusiastic handshake during the 1940 World Series.

Bucky Walters *(left)* and Billy Werber. Bucky has just won his second game of the 1940 Series, tying the affair at three games apiece.

Cincinnati welcoming its conquering heroes after the 1940 World Series victory.

nati had its first world title since the dubious victory of 1919. The 2–1 finale was fitting for a club that had won 41 1-run games during the season.

Cincinnati was a bedlam of excitement and celebration; in some quarters it went on for days. Toasted over and over were Walters and Derringer, winners of two Series games apiece; Werber, with 10 hits and a .370 batting average; Ripple, with a .333 average and 6 runs batted in; and the tough old catcher Wilson, who caught all seven games, batted .353, and had the only stolen base of the Series.

Cincinnati had waited 19 years for their first pennant, 20 for their second, then immediately won a third. The wait for flag number four, however, would be a long 21 years.

T▾E▾N

THE LONG WAIT BEGINS

THE Reds, like the rest of the National League, were spectators to a thrilling Dodger-Cardinal pennant race in 1941 that saw Brooklyn finish on top for the first time in 21 years. The Cincinnati club that came in third in 1941, 12 games out, differed little from the world champions of 1940. Billy Myers had been traded to the Cubs for outfielder Jim Gleeson and Eddie Joost became the regular shortstop. Otherwise, the club lined up in familiar places, but not with the same productivity.

Frank McCormick, beginning to suffer from the back problems that were to hamper his career, slumped to .269; Lombardi, to .264. The team's leading hitter was Mike McCormick at .287, marking the first time since 1914 the Reds were without a .300 hitter. Walters was 19–15, and Derringer, a disappointing 12–14. Vander Meer was 16–13 with 202 league-leading strikeouts, but the surprise ace was Elmer Riddle, who had pitched sparingly in relief the year before. The right-hander won his first 11 decisions and ended with a glittering 19–4 record and the lowest ERA in the league, 2.24.

Elmer Riddle won 19 games for the Reds in 1941 and 21 in 1943. He pitched for the Reds from 1939 through 1945 and in 1947.

The breakup of the world championship team continued after the season. Werber was sold to the Giants and Lombardi to the Braves. The usually mild-mannered Ernie had publicly called Giles "a cheapskate" after a salary dispute and this lapse in diplomacy probably moved Giles to sell his star catcher. (Ernie batted .330 for the Braves in 1942 and won his second batting title.)

By this time, however, the city of Cincinnati, along with the rest of the country, had other things on its mind. On December 7, 1941, the Japanese attack on Pearl Harbor had brought America into the war that had been drawing blood since September 1939. Before long, scouting reports were including, along with talent evaluations, a man's standing with the draft board, although the full impact of war-related roster depletions would not be felt until 1943.

Ernie Lombardi.

The Reds came in fourth in 1942, this time with a revamped team. While Frank McCormick, Frey, and Joost remained in place, McKechnie had Bert Haas at third and a new outfield of Max Marshall, Eric Tipton, and former American League star Gerald ("Gee") Walker. Rookie Ray Lamanno did the bulk of the catching. McCormick's .277 average was the highest on a team that batted a collective .231, lowest in the league since 1910.

Vander Meer at 18–12 was the ace, again leading in strikeouts with 186. Ray Starr, a veteran minor leaguer, was added to the staff and came through with a 15–13 record, Walters was 15–14. Derringer, in decline, was 10–11 and was sold to the Cubs after the season. Riddle, 1941's ace, slumped to 7–11.

Along with Derringer, other postseason departures included Goodman, also to the Cubs, and Joost to the Braves in a deal that brought the Reds Eddie Miller, a light hitter but one of the fine fielding shortstops of the time.

With wartime travel restrictions now in force, baseball teams were unable to go south for spring training. So, beginning in 1943, for the next three springs the Reds used the Indiana University facilities at Bloomington, employing the field house when the weather did not permit outdoor workouts. (This arrangement was to pay a huge dividend. In 1945, the club spotted and signed a muscular youngster named Ted Kluszewski, at the time attending the university on a football scholarship and also playing on the baseball team.)

Thanks to some sturdy pitching, McKechnie brought his club in third in 1943, although this is not to suggest there was a pennant race—the Cardinals were first by 18 games. Riddle returned to form with a 21–11 record, Walters was 15–15, and Vander Meer (the strikeout leader for the third straight season with 174) was 15–16. Southpaw Clyde Shoun, obtained from the Cardinals the year before, was 14–5. Frank McCormick's .303 average was the team's best. With Ray Lamanno then in the navy, the catching was handled by a tough, sturdy veteran, Ray Mueller, who had previously been with the Braves and Pirates.

Eddie Joost (1936–1937, 1939–1942), who replaced Billy Myers at shortstop for the Reds.

Cincinnati's Eddie Joost has just forced Brooklyn's Joe Medwick at second and is firing on to first. Lonny Frey is watching the play as umpire Bill Stewart gives the "out" call.

Lonny Frey, Cincinnati's popular second baseman.

Johnny Vander Meer (1937–1943, 1946–1949). The double no-hit man also led in strikeouts three straight years. His top winning season was 18 in 1942.

Eddie Miller (1936–1937, 1943–1947), one of the most gifted defensive shortstops of his era.

Ray Starr (1941–1943) was a 15-game winner in 1942.

Utility third baseman Chuck Aleno (1941–1944).

Harry Craft.

Reserve catcher Dick West (1938–1943).

Outfielder Ernie Koy (1941–1942), whose native American ancestry earned him the usual nickname of "Chief."

That's Lonny Frey waiting for the peg as New York's Dick Bartell is stealing second. The ball skipped through and Bartell was safe. The action occurred at the Polo Grounds in May 1942.

Gerald Walker (1942–1945), a veteran American Leaguer who helped fill out Cincinnati's outfield during the war years.

Infielder Woody Williams, who got into only thirty games for the Reds that year, rapped himself into the record books with a few days of steady hitting. On September 4 he went 4 for 4 against the Cardinals. After an off day, he went 5 for 5 in the first game of a doubleheader against the Cubs, then made it ten hits in a row in the second game (nine singles and a double) before being stopped. He remains tied with seven other hitters (five in this century) for the National League record for consecutive hits.

Over the next two seasons, 1944 and 1945, big-league rosters resembled so many patched tires. Any healthy and eligible male between the ages of eighteen and thirty-eight was subject to the call of the selective service board. Those left behind were "either too young or too old" (in the lyrics of a popular wartime song) or were suffering from one disability or another that made them unfit for military service.

Cincinnati players who lost time to the military included Beggs, Thompson, Vander Meer, Shoun, and Harry Gumbert among the pitchers, catchers Lamanno and Mueller, in-

Ray Lamanno (1941–1942, 1946–1948), whose big-league career was sliced down the middle by military service.

Clyde Shoun (1942–1944, 1946–1947), a tough left-hander, was called "Hardrock." He was 14–5 in 1943.

Game time at Crosley Field in 1943.

fielders Frey and Haas, and outfielders Mike McCormick, Clyde Vollmer, and Max Marshall.

McKechnie's men finished third in 1944, led by a 23–8 season from the veteran Walters. Frank McCormick led the team with a .305 average. They were the only players left from the 1940 world champions, many of whom were now scattered throughout outposts and fighting fronts around the world.

There are two prominent symbols of baseball's wartime barrel scraping: the St. Louis Browns' one-armed outfielder Pete Gray, and the youth the Reds put on the mound on June 10, 1944. He was a strapping left-hander named Joe Nuxhall, a Hamilton, Ohio, high-school student who was seven weeks short of his sixteenth birthday (he needed special permission to sign a contract), making him the youngest big leaguer to play in this century. The boy was put into a hopelessly lost game with the Cardinals, pitched two-thirds of an inning, allowed 2 hits and 5 bases on balls, then departed. He would later make his way back and enjoy a long and productive big-league career.

The flip side of the Nuxhall coin was Clyde Shoun's 1–0 no-hitting of the Braves on May 15, 1944, a day after Walters had 1-hit the same club. Also on the positive side was the work of Ray Mueller, who set a league record by catching every one of the club's 155 games (135 of them complete).

After seven straight first-division finishes under McKechnie, the Reds dropped to seventh place in 1945, beginning what would become a stretch of 11 straight second-division nestings, matching the 1927–1937 twilight.

With the war over and the big-league regulars back in place, the fifty-nine-year-old McKechnie began his ninth and final season as manager of the Cincinnati Reds. It was a disappointing one—sixth place and a league-low .239 batting average.

With Frank McCormick having been sold to the Phillies, Bert Haas was at first base, newcomer Bobby Adams shared second with Frey, Miller was at short, and rookie Grady Hatton was at third. Hatton had never played in the minors, but had done so well with service teams during the war that he was given a shot in spring training and made the team.

Ray Mueller (1943–1944, 1946–1949), Cincinnati's "Iron Man" behind the plate, who appeared in 155 games in 1944.

Paul Derringer.

He did well, batting .271. Mueller was back behind the plate, but the outfield of Al Libke, Dain Clay, and Eddie Lukon was weak. Joe Beggs, turned into a starter, was the top winner at 12–10. The most talented man on the staff, however, was a 6-foot, 6-inch right-hander with a whiplash sidearm delivery that had right-handed hitters muttering. Ewell Blackwell had appeared in two games with the Reds in 1942, then had gone into the army and marched through Europe with Patton's Third Army. Now he was back and al-

Frank McCormick.

though posting just a 9–13 record, had a league-high 6 shutouts and 2.47 ERA.

On September 22, it was announced that McKechnie was leaving the club. Deacon Bill's nine-year tenure as skipper was the longest in Reds history (Sparky Anderson would later tie it), and overall it had been a successful one: There had been seven first-division finishes, two pennants, and one world championship.

Bert Haas (1942–1943, 1946–1947), who played first, third, and the outfield for the Reds.

About ten days later, Giles announced that the new manager would be Johnny Neun, a forty-six-year-old former major-league first baseman and long-time minor-league manager for the Yankees, for whom he was coaching when hired by Giles. Neun's big-league playing career, split between the Detroit Tigers and Boston Braves, had been forgettable except for one lustrous moment. On May 31, 1927, while playing for Detroit, he executed that rarest of baseball stunners, the unassisted triple play.

"It's like being hit by lightning," Neun said whimsically of his great moment. "If you're not standing in just the right place, nothing's going to happen."

Later the league's MVP as a relief pitcher for the Phillies, Jim Konstanty pitched for the Reds as a starter and reliever in 1944, posting a 6–4 record.

Bill McKechnie *(left)* and pitcher Joe Nuxhall in June 1944, when Joe was not quite sixteen years old.

In what was to prove to be Neun's only full season, the Reds came in fifth, with Ewell Blackwell filling an otherwise dull season with plenty of excitement. The broomstick-thin right-hander suddenly emerged as baseball's most exciting pitcher. Tall and rangy, with a sidearm delivery that unwound and snapped like a whip, Blackwell astonished and entertained the universe of baseball with 16 consecutive victories, the league's longest 1-season winning streak since New York's Rube Marquard had 19 in 1912. And in the midst of it, he made a breathtaking grasp for the most glittering star in the pitching firmament.

Manager Johnny Neun *(left)* welcoming his new first baseman, Babe Young in June 1947.

On June 18, Blackwell no-hit the Braves, winning 6–0 on a pair of three-run homers struck by first baseman Babe Young, who had been acquired from the Giants (in exchange for Joe Beggs). This was the ninth straight win in Blackwell's streak. Four days later, he went after number ten against the Brooklyn Dodgers.

As Blackwell turned in inning after inning of hitless ball, the similarities between his effort and Vander Meer's double no-hitters of 1938 became more and more compelling. Like Blackwell, Vander Meer had turned out his gems in June, and against the same clubs, first Boston and then Brooklyn. And adding a dramatic fillip to the occasion, there was Johnny himself, still in a Cincinnati uniform, watching from the dugout.

"If he had done it," Vander Meer said, "I was going to be the first one out there to congratulate him."

Blackwell went far in his mighty effort, to one out in the ninth inning. At that point the slap-hitting Eddie Stanky rammed a shot right back through Blackwell's legs and into center field for a clean single.

Ed Heusser (1943–1946), one of the bulwarks of Cincinnati's wartime pitching staff, was the ERA leader in 1944.

"It wasn't hit as hard as I thought," Blackwell said later, "and I went down for it too quickly. I thought I had the ball and lifted my glove up too soon and the damned thing went right under it. And that was that."

Blackwell subsequently yielded another hit to Jackie Robinson and had to be satisfied with a 2-hit victory. The 16-game winning streak lasted until July 30, when the Giants beat him in ten innings, 5–4.

The story of Cincinnati's 1947 season is the story of Ewell Blackwell. When the bats had been stacked in the autumn shadows, the Reds ace was 22–8, leading the league in wins, strikeouts (193), and complete games (23).

Injuries and illness dropped Blackwell to a 7–9 record in 1948, and the club dropped with him, to seventh place, their .247 team batting average the league's worst. Vander Meer churned out his last big season (17–14) and Cincinnati native Herman Wehmeier, a twenty-one-year-old right-hander, was 11–8.

With Eddie Miller traded to the Phillies for outfielder Johnny Wyrostek, the Reds broke in Virgil Stallcup at shortstop, a job he would hold down for four years. In the outfield, the

Ewell Blackwell (1942, 1946–1952).

Backup catcher Al Lakeman (1942–1947).

Primarily a reliever, Johnny Hetki pitched for the Reds from 1945 to 1948 and in 1950.

In 1947 Ewell Blackwell was spectacular.

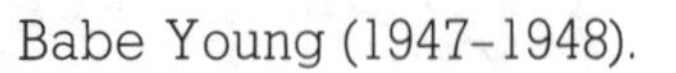

Babe Young (1947–1948).

That's Ray Lamanno trying to catch up to a pop foul at the edge of the Philadelphia Phillies dugout. He didn't make the catch. The action occurred at Shibe Park in June 1947.

team suddenly had a first-class bombardier in Hank Sauer. The big slugger had had previous trials with the Reds and now, at the age of thirty-one, he exploded. His 35 home runs set a new club record. And at first base now was the former Indiana University football player, Ted Kluszewski, batting .274 and hitting 12 home runs. Klu, by his own telling, was a spray hitter when he first came up, hitting the ball where it was pitched. Fearful of

A well-seasoned veteran by the time he joined the Reds, outfielder Augie Galan (1947–1948) gave the club a .314 year in 1947.

Bucky Walters.

Crosley Field in repose.

Right-hander Harry Gumbert (1944, 1946–1949), who made 61 relief appearances for the Reds in 1948, most in the league.

Hank Sauer (1941–1942, 1945, 1948–1949), who hit 35 home runs in 1948, a year before he was traded to the Cubs.

Third baseman Grady Hatton (1946–1954) got to the majors without any minor-league experience.

Utility infielder Benny Zientara (1941, 1946–1948).

Outfielder Frank Baumholtz (1947–1949) batted .296 in 1948.

(LEFT) Virgil Stallcup (1947–1952), for four years Cincinnati's regular shortstop.

(BELOW LEFT) Southpaw Kent Peterson (1944, 1947–1951) never quite fulfilled the expectations the Reds had of him.

(BELOW) Eddie Erautt (1947–1951, 1953) worked primarily in relief for the Reds.

Right-hander Howie Fox (1944–1946, 1948–1951). His 19 losses led the league in 1949.

to be ready to talk to the press after every game, win or lose."

For skipper Bucky, there were far more losses to talk about than wins; in 1949 the club was 62–92, and at the end of the season, Walters was let out and replaced by Luke Sewell. Luke was a long-time American League catcher who in 1944 had managed the St. Louis Browns to the only pennant that team ever won.

On June 15, 1949 the Reds, disenchanted with the slow start Sauer was off to, had traded their big power hitter along with outfielder Frankie Baumholtz to the Cubs in exchange for outfielders Peanuts Lowrey and Harry Walker. It was not a good trade for the Reds, as neither Lowrey nor Walker lasted in Cincinnati beyond the following season, while Sauer went on to give the Cubs a

his great power, pitchers were inclined to work him outside. This led to many line drives through the box.

"After I'd picked a number of them off the hill," Kluszewski said, "they began pitching me inside, figuring the hell with it, they'd rather take a chance on giving up the long ball than getting brained. So when you look at my record and see how my home run count suddenly jumped, that accounts for it. They were pitching me inside and I was going with it."

The club's poor showing in 1948 was a sluggish tide that finally carried Neun out of his job; on August 6, 1948, Johnny was fired and Bucky Walters hired. The thirty-nine-year-old pitcher's superb playing career had run its course (he retired with a 198–160 record), and now he was manager, a job he never felt comfortable in.

"I never cared for managing," he said. "When I was pitching, if I lost a game I could go sit by myself in the clubhouse and nobody would bother me. But as a manager, I'd have

Walker Cooper caught for six National League teams during his long career, stopping off in Cincinnati for parts of the 1949 and 1950 seasons.

Outfielder Johnny Wyrostek (1948–1952). He batted .311 in 1951.

half dozen years of superior home run hitting (he was MVP in 1952).

Another 1949 acquisition who remained with the Reds only briefly was veteran catcher Walker Cooper, who was there long enough to put on what is probably the most devastating 1-game hitting display in club history. Against the Cubs at Crosley Field on July 6, Cooper was 6 for 6, with 3 home runs, 3 singles, 10 runs batted in, and 5 runs scored, leading a 23–4 rubout of the Cubs.

Outside of the Cooper explosion, the Reds went into the books fairly quietly in 1949. Curveballing left-hander Ken Raffensberger was the mainstay of the staff with an 18–17 record.

The decade that had begun with a world championship ended with the team idling in seventh place, with nothing but arid years ahead. Nevertheless—and who could have known it?—the seedlings of a glorious era were already sprouting here and there. Living right under the Reds' noses in Cincinnati was an energetic eight-year-old named Peter Edward Rose. And down in Oklahoma was a robust two-year-old named Johnny Lee Bench. And further down, in Texas, was a bright little six-year-old named Joe Leonard Morgan. And further away, enjoying the warm Caribbean breezes that crossed his native Cuba, was a cheerful seven-year-old named Atanasio Perez. And even further off, in Venezuela, taking his first steps was one-year-old David Concepcion.

From little Tinker Toys grow Big Red Machines.

E·L·E·V·E·N

STILL WAITING

WHEN the Reds finally came out of the 1950s doldrums it would be thunderously—record shatteringly thunderous, in fact. But before the excitement, a long, slow road had to be trod. More to the point, for four years, 1950-1953, there was no movement at all. As if they had signed a lease, the club spent those years moldering in sixth place, unable to go either backward or forward. So fixed and immutable was their situation that they played to almost identical records in these four straight seasons: 66–87, 68–86, 69–85, 68–86.

On February 10, 1950, Johnny Vander Meer, the last member of the 1940 world champions still with the team, was sold to the Cubs. In Ted Kluszewski, the team had its only star of the future, the big first baseman batting .307, with 25 home runs and 111 RBIs. The club had brought up a good-hitting rookie in Joe Adcock, who batted .293 in 102 games. But the twenty-two-year-old power hitter presented the Reds with a problem. By ability and inclination, Joe was a first baseman, but with Kluszewski anchored at the bag (and not possessing the mobility to play elsewhere), the new man was put in the outfield, where he was not happy. After three years the Reds solved the problem the only way they could, by trading Adcock. Joe went to Milwaukee, took over the first base job and went on to years of productive long-ball hitting.

Recovered from his variety of miseries, Blackwell came back with a 17–15 record in 1950, although he would never again be the dominating pitcher he was in 1947. Raffensberger with his pinpoint curves (40 walks in 239 innings) was 14–19.

Ted Kluszewski (1947-1957), one of the greatest and most popular of all Cincinnati players.

Sewell's 1951 sixth-place finishers had the league's lowest team average (.248) and scored the fewest runs (559), and only Black-

Joe Adcock (1950–1952). He preferred playing first base, but the Reds also had Kluszewski.

Ken Raffensberger (1947–1954), one of the Reds' steadier winners in the early 1950s.

Luke Sewell, Reds manager from 1950 to 1952.

Shortstop Roy McMillan (1951–1960), "one of the most magical gloves ever seen at the position."

well (16–15) and Raffensberger (16–17) kept them out of last place. Roy McMillan, a twenty-year-old shortshop with one of the most magical gloves ever seen at the position, began replacing Stallcup.

It was at the end of the 1951 season that Warren Giles was elected president of the National League. Giles's successor was his long-time assistant Gabe Paul. The forty-year-old Paul was one of the most gifted men ever to work in a baseball executive suite. He had started in 1926, just sixteen years old, working as a publicity man for the Rochester club of the International League and would remain in the game until 1984, when he re-

Bobby Adams, who gave the Reds some sharp play at second and third from 1946 to 1955. He generally batted around .270.

(RIGHT) Connie Ryan, who gave the Reds some snappy work at second base in 1950–1951.

Rogers Hornsby managed the Reds in 1952 and 1953 and seemed to go out of his way to prove that great hitters don't necessarily make great managers.

Outfielder Lloyd Merriman (1949–1951, 1954), whose speed afoot earned him the nickname "Citation" after the champion racehorse of the day.

tired as president of the Cleveland Indians, along the way working for the Reds, the Houston Astros, and the New York Yankees.

The 1952 club, still on its sixth-place treadmill, made a managerial change on July 28, letting Sewell go and replacing him with Rogers Hornsby. It was to prove one of Paul's few mistakes.

Hornsby remains baseball's greatest right-handed hitter, three times batting over .400 as a second baseman with the Cardinals in the 1920s (where he managed the club to a world championship in 1926) and compiling a lifetime average of .358. But as a manager, Rogers was a long-proven dud, having worn out welcomes with the Boston Braves, Chicago Cubs, and St. Louis Browns, the latter on two occasions.

Hornsby was an arrogant and sarcastic man, brusque and impatient with his players. Also, he sometimes lost track of where his priorities lay. Grady Hatton recalled one occasion when the skipper was giving pregame batting tips to the opposing players, who, like everyone else in baseball, were mesmerized by the Hornsby aura and had begun talking hitting with the great man during batting practice.

"It was an unbelievable sight," Hatton said. "There's our manager standing behind the batting cage giving the other guys tips on how to hit."

The brightest lights on the 1952 team were Kluszewski (.320) and Raffensberger (17–13), with right-hander Frank Smith turning in some first-rate relief work.

The year's low point came on May 21 at Ebbets Field, when the Reds had to suffer through a 15-run first inning by the Dodgers, during which 19 consecutive Dodgers reached base safely. Blackwell, who started for the Reds, was quickly KO'd; he showered and took a cab back to the team's Manhattan hotel. When he walked into the bar, he recalled, the game was on television.

"I sat down to have a drink," Blackwell said, "and asked the bartender what inning they were in. He said it was still the bottom of the first. Then the guy who had relieved me, Bud Byerly, came in and sat down and asked what inning it was. I told him to forget it."

Frank Smith (1950–1954, 1956), a top reliever in the early 1950s.

(Struggling with a 3–12 record, Blackwell was dealt to the Yankees at the end of August.)

Brooding all summer long under the unpopular Hornsby, the Reds again ran sixth in 1953. But this time the club had some punch. The home run, long absent from the team's arsenal, had arrived at Crosley Field. Kluszewski erupted with 40 (with 108 RBIs), outfielder Gus Bell had 30 (105 RBIs), out-

Jim Greengrass *(left)* and Herman Wehmeier celebrating a Reds victory in 1952. Greengrass (1952–1955) was a power-hitting outfielder and Wehmeier (1945, 1947–1954), a regular starter for a half dozen years.

fielder Jim Greengrass had 20 (100 RBIs), and catcher Andy Seminick had 19. Bell had been acquired from the Pirates in one of Paul's best deals, Greengrass had come from the Yankee farm system in the Blackwell deal, and Seminick had been obtained from the Phillies. Overall, the club banged out 166 home runs, a new Cincinnati record.

The Reds were emancipated at the end of the season when Paul fired Hornsby and re-

Bud Byerly (1950–1952), who gave the Reds some good bullpen work.

placed him with former American League catcher George ("Birdie") Tebbetts, a forty-two-year-old chatterbox with a high-pitched voice (hence his nickname) and a solid reputation in baseball circles.

Tebbetts moved the gears in 1954, and after four years of sixth-place languishing, the club moved up one notch with a 74–80 record, their highest win total since 1944.

On April 17, 1954, outfielder Nino Escalera became the first black to play for the Reds in a regular season game. The Puerto Rican–born Escalera was followed to the plate by

The rugged catcher Andy Seminick (1952–1955) hit 19 homers in 1953.

Birdie Tebbets, Reds manager from 1954 to 1958.

outfielder Chuck Harmon, who was the first American-born black to play in a Cincinnati uniform. Aside from their places in history, neither man made much impact at Crosley Field.

The charge into fifth place was led by the heavy bombing of Kluszewski, who set new team records with 49 home runs and 141 runs batted in. He was the first Cincinnati player since Fred Odwell in 1905 to lead the league in four baggers. Kluszewski hit his 49th home run on September 16, then set his sights on the big number five-oh.

Second baseman Johnny Temple (1952–1959, 1964) batted .311 for the Reds in 1959.

"I never swung for home runs," Klu said, "but I really wanted that fiftieth. But I never got it. I'd hit forty-nine without trying and then when I tried I couldn't do it, game after game. Is there a moral in there somewhere?"

Greengrass backed up big Klu with 27 homers and Gus Bell had 17. The club also added another longballer in outfielder Wally Post, a man with a strong arm, a haymaker swing (he led the league in strikeouts three times), and lots of power. The Ohio native broke in with 18 homers.

At second base the club now had the hustling, hard-nosed Johnny Temple (batting .307). The club's top pitcher was left-hander

Chuck Harmon (1954–1955), Cincinnati's first American-born black player.

Joe Nuxhall (12–5), the same Nuxhall who had made history in 1944 when he took the mound before his sixteenth birthday. Joe had worked his way back in 1952 as a reliever, began starting in 1953 (when he was 9–11) and now, a decade after his historic debut, had come full cycle as the club's most successful pitcher.

The Reds stayed in place in 1955, staking out the fifth slot once more, but again with a lot of power, depositing 181 souvenirs around the league. Kluszewski hit 47 of them, establishing a National League record for most home runs in two consecutive seasons by a left-handed hitter, 96. Klu and three teammates accounted for 134 of the club's 181 muscle shots, Post hitting 40; Bell, 27; and catcher Smoky Burgess, 20. Never the most adept of catchers, Burgess (acquired from the Phillies in April 1955 in a trade that saw Seminick and Greengrass go east) was a 5-foot, 8-inch stump of natural hitting propensities. (His 145 lifetime pinch hits are second to Manny Mota's 150 on the all-time list.) The team's .270 batting average was topped in the league only by Brooklyn's .271, with Kluszewski, Post, Bell, and Burgess all over .300.

Pitching, of course, was the problem in 1955. Nuxhall (17–12) was the only successful starter on the staff (in addition to starting thirty-three games, Nuxhall was pressed into relief seventeen times by the pitching-poor Tebbetts). Right-hander Hersh Freeman, an

Crosley Field's left-field wall.

Jim Greengrass.

(LEFT) Outfielder Willard Marshall (1952–1953) hit 17 homers in 1953.

(ABOVE) Harry Perkowski (1947, 1949–1954), who was a 12-game winner for the Reds in 1952 and 1953.

(LEFT) Jackie Collum, who started and relieved for the Reds from 1953 to 1955.

Right-hander Bud Podbielan (1952–1955, 1957).

Ted Kluszewski.

Rocky Bridges (1953–1957), a hustling and personable utility infielder. He invented the "hernia hit"—looping fly balls that infielders strained themselves reaching for.

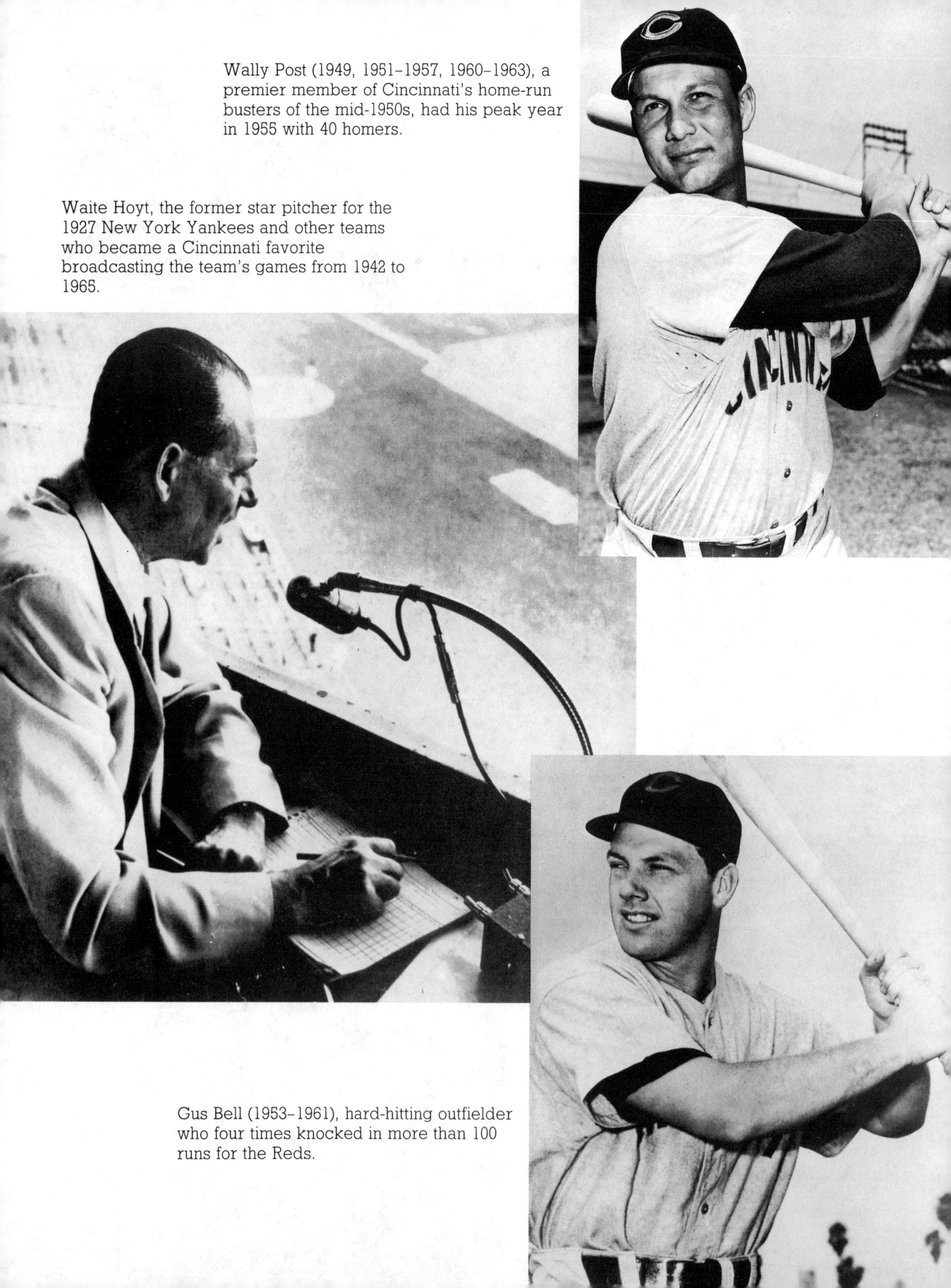

Wally Post (1949, 1951–1957, 1960–1963), a premier member of Cincinnati's home-run busters of the mid-1950s, had his peak year in 1955 with 40 homers.

Waite Hoyt, the former star pitcher for the 1927 New York Yankees and other teams who became a Cincinnati favorite broadcasting the team's games from 1942 to 1965.

Gus Bell (1953–1961), hard-hitting outfielder who four times knocked in more than 100 runs for the Reds.

Ted Kluszewski scoring the hard way. The catcher is New York's Bob Schmidt, the umpire Jocko Conlan. The action occurred at the Polo Grounds in 1955.

early-season pickup from the Red Sox, gave the club some superb relief innings.

Although not reflected in the team's fifth-place finish, the Reds ran off a 12-game May winning streak that equaled the best in their modern history.

The 1956 season is remembered in Cincinnati as one of the most exciting in club annals. Not only did the team break out of its eleven-year second-division straitjacket and set a new attendance mark of 1,125,928 but it also tied the major-league home-run record and came within touching distance of a pennant no one ever expected it to contend for.

The Reds' already powerful lineup was augmented by the addition of hard-hitting catcher Ed Bailey and the young outfielder who was to become, by general agreement, the greatest player in the history of the Cincinnati franchise, Frank Robinson.

Robinson was born in Beaumont, Texas, but grew up in Oakland, where the Reds discovered him and signed him as soon as the youngster had graduated high school. Following three seasons of minor-league apprenticeship, Robinson, just twenty years old, went to spring training with the Reds in 1956 and made the team.

Catcher Smoky Burgess (1955–1958), who batted .306 for the Reds in 1955.

Art Fowler (1954–1956), his best was 12–10 in 1954.

Joe Nuxhall (1944, 1952–1960, 1962–1966), the youngest man ever to play big-league baseball. He later became one of the Reds' star pitchers and finally a popular member of its broadcast crew.

Hersh Freeman (1955–1958), who gave the Reds some excellent relief work.

"Robinson," said an appreciative Ted Kluszewski, "was one tough kid right from the get-go. He had an unusual stance. He really crowded the plate. Sometimes he leaned right out over it. Naturally, he was thrown at a lot; he was forever getting hit or going down. But it never bothered him. He'd get right back up and dig right back in." Kluszewski went on to say that Robinson "had a fire in him, from the very beginning."

Getting some unexpectedly strong pitching from right-hander Brooks Lawrence (acquired from the Cardinals in a minor trade), who won his first thirteen decisions, the Reds suddenly found themselves in a pennant race with the Brooklyn Dodgers and Milwaukee Braves.

No Cincinnati team—in fact, very few teams ever—hit home runs like this one did. On August 18, the Reds tied a National League record by popping 8 homers in one game against Milwaukee. The perpetrators were reserve outfielder Bob Thurman (who had 3), Kluszewski and Robinson (2 each), and Post.

The Reds remained amid the clouds of excitement, a few games from the top, until a 4-game losing streak in mid-September that proved fatal. Despite winning 8 of their last

Ed Bailey, Cincinnati's hard-hitting catcher, who was with the club from 1953 to 1961. He hit 28 homers in 1956.

Frank Robinson (1956–1965), "by general agreement, the greatest player in the history of the Cincinnati franchise."

Brooks Lawrence (1956–1960), a 19-game winner in 1956.

A well-traveled right-hander, Johnny Klippstein's itinerary included stops in Cincinnati in 1955–1958 and 1962. He both started and relieved for the Reds.

9, they could never make up the tantalizing few games that separated them from the promised land and finished with a 91–63 record, 1 game behind second-place Milwaukee and 2 behind the pennant-winning Dodgers.

The exciting, disappointing season ended on a parting shot of glory: on September 29, in the club's next-to-last game, Smoky Burgess hit the team's 221st and last home run of the year, tying the major-league record set by the 1947 New York Giants (the 1961 Yankees are the current record holders with 240).

Five Reds players had upper-echelon home run totals: Robinson (38), Post (36), Kluszewski (35), Bell (29), and Bailey (28), with Klu and Bailey each batting just over .300. Robinson's total tied the major-league record

The good-hitting Jerry Lynch (1957–1963), who played part-time in the outfield and did some lusty pinch hitting.

First baseman George Crowe (1956–1958) hit 31 home runs for the Reds in 1956.

for rookies (since broken) set by Wally Berger in 1930. The Reds hit 44 of their home runs against the Dodgers, setting the National League record for homers against one club. The team's 775 runs led the league.

Cincinnati, however, had come up short on the mound. Where the Dodgers had Don Newcombe, Sal Maglie, Carl Erskine, and Roger Craig, and Milwaukee had three big winners in Warren Spahn, Lew Burdette, and

That's Roy McMillan making a midair delivery after forcing Brooklyn's Rube Walker at second.

Bob Buhl, the Reds had but one ace in Lawrence, who was 19–10 (6–10 after winning his first 13), and then Nuxhall (13–11) and Johnny Klippstein (12–11). Hersh Freeman again delivered strong bullpen work, going 14–5 and saving 18.

After the season, Robinson was the unanimous choice for Rookie of the Year, the first Cincinnati player to win the award.

The 1957 club again hit hard—187 home runs—but finished fourth. A bad back restricted Kluszewski to just sixty-nine games (the popular Klu was traded to Pittsburgh after the season), but George Crowe filled in adequately, hitting 31 homers and driving in 91 runs. Temple and McMillan continued turning out snazzy double plays, and third baseman Don Hoak, obtained from the Cubs, hit a surprising .293. Robinson batted .322, with 29 home runs, while Bell hit just 13, and Post (who was traded to the Phillies for left-hander Harvey Haddix in December

1957) clubbed just 20. Curiously, Wally had peaked at the age of twenty-seven and was never the same masher after that.

Lawrence again was the big winner, this time with a 16–13 mark. Freeman, after several fine years, became spotty in relief and had to be picked up by Klippstein and right-hander Tom Acker.

In a case of ballot box stuffing flagrant enough to warm the heart of a jaded old ward heeler, Reds fans voted eight of their heroes onto the National League All-Star team: Bailey, Crowe, Temple, McMillan, Hoak, Robinson, Bell, and Post. This affront to electoral propriety was corrected by Commissioner Ford Frick, who scrubbed Crowe, Post, and Bell (replacing them with gentlemen named Stan Musial, Henry Aaron, and Willie Mays).

Tom Acker, who turned in some fine relief work for the Reds from 1956 to 1959.

Feisty third baseman Don Hoak (1957–1958).

Bell was later added to the squad as a substitute.

In 1958 the Reds got off poorly and continued to stumble; by the third week in July they were in last place. As the slump continued, a discouraged Tebbetts resigned on August 14 and was replaced by coach Jimmy Dykes. The personable Dykes had previously managed the Chicago White Sox, Philadelphia Athletics, and Baltimore Orioles, and would later manage the Detroit Tigers and Cleveland Indians (in all, twenty-one years of brainstorming and three third-place finishes to show for it). Jimmy steered the ship of state into more placid waters, posting a 24–17 rec-

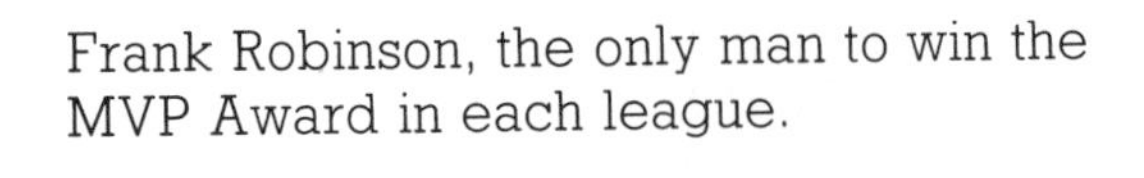

Frank Robinson, the only man to win the MVP Award in each league.

ord, good enough to nudge the club into fourth place at the bell. Despite his good showing, Jimmy was replaced after the season by Mayo Smith, formerly manager of the Phillies.

The 1958 Reds slipped to 123 homers, led by Robinson's 31. Rookie outfielder Jerry Lynch, drafted from the Pacific Coast League, was a pleasant surprise, batting .312. Temple was a .306 hitter, but Bell, Crowe, and Bailey slipped badly.

Right-hander Bob Purkey, acquired from Pittsburgh, topped the staff with a 17–11 record. Nuxhall (12–11) was the only other

Frank Robinson is on third and Don Hoak is trying to drive him in.

(ABOVE LEFT) Utility outfielder Pete Whisenant (1957–1961).

(ABOVE RIGHT) Vada Pinson (1958–1968), a .316 hitter in his rookie year.

pitcher to win in double figures. Don Newcombe, a midseason pickup from the Dodgers—who, like the Giants, were now posted in California—was a disappointment, the former Cy Young award winner breaking even at 7–7.

The Reds brought up a gem of a rookie that year in twenty-year-old outfielder Vada Pinson (he had got into a handful of games in 1958). The compact youngster was in command of all the tools of stardom: hitting

Don Newcombe (1958–1960), who was just past his prime when the Reds got him.

Young southpaw Claude Osteen (1957, 1959–1961), whom the Reds let get away; he went on to win 196 major-league games.

ability with more than average power, defensive prowess, a good arm, and terrific speed. While Pinson never quite attained the superstardom that was predicted for him, his manifold abilities were good enough to sustain an 18-year big-league career (the first 11 spent with the Reds), during which he averaged .286 and rapped out 2,757 hits.

Pinson's arrival crowded the Reds outfield and pushed Frank Robinson to first base, a position he handled for a year and a half. No matter where he played, Robinson hit, in 1959 whacking 36 home runs, driving in 125 runs, and batting .311. Temple also batted .311, and young Pinson broke in at .316. Pinson's 205 hits made him the fourth player in Reds history to get 200 or more hits in a season (the others were Cy Seymour, Jake Daubert, and Frank McCormick), and his 131 runs led the league and set a new club record (broken by Robinson's 134 in 1962).

The 1959 Reds finished a disappointing sixth, despite leading the league in batting (.274) and runs (764), and making the second fewest errors (126). So the finger of guilt once more pointed to the pitching staff. Newcombe was the leader with a 13–8 record and Purkey was 13–18, the only double-figure winners on a mound corps that logged a 4.31 ERA, sixth worst in the league. To make matters worse, the club had in its grasp two young left-handers whom they let get away and whom were to spend long and productive careers elsewhere: Claude Osteen and Mike Cuellar.

On July 8, with the team loitering in seventh place, Smith was fired and replaced by Fred Hutchinson. Of Gabe Paul's previous three managerial appointments, two were unsuccessful (Hornsby and Smith) and one was successful (Tebbets). Hutchinson was to prove one of Gabe's better selections.

Infielder Eddie Kasko (1959–1963). His best was .292 in 1960.

T·W·E·L·V·E

A PENNANT FOR THE SIXTIES

WHEN he pitched for the Detroit Tigers in the 1940s and early 1950s, Fred Hutchinson was known as one of baseball's most uncompromising competitors and hardest losers; a tough Hutchinson defeat was known to lead to the rearrangement of clubhouse furniture. When his pitching days were brought to premature conclusion by a bad arm, Hutch's acknowledged leadership qualities led him to managerial posts at Detroit and with the St. Louis Cardinals, who let him out at the end of the 1958 season.

Hutchinson was as volatile a manager as he had been a player. The big man (6 feet, 2 inches and 190 pounds) had a short-leashed temper that could be explosive. Managers of this disposition are often disliked by their players; Hutchinson, however, was a more complete personality. Beneath his tempestuous exterior was a man of warmth, character, and sly humor. His players respected him and liked him.

Hutchinson's first year as Reds manager, 1960, proved to be a transitional one. The pitching was bolstered by the development of left-hander Jim O'Toole (12–12) and reliever Jim Brosnan, a big right-hander acquired the previous summer from the Cardinals. Brosnan was bright and witty and would soon turn out a pair of diary-styled reminiscences, *The Long Season* and *Pennant Race,* that have become permanent parts of baseball literature. Just joining the staff was twenty-year-old Jim Maloney, a right-hander who threw with exceptional speed.

The club began breaking Leo Cardenas in

Fred Hutchinson, Reds manager from 1959 to 1964.

The tough and talented left-hander Jim O'Toole (1958–1966) won 19 in 1961.

Right-handed reliever Jim Brosnan (1959–1963), who also has a pair of classics of baseball literature to his credit.

Shortstop Chico Cardenas (1960–1968).

Gordon Coleman (1960–1968) parked 28 homers in 1962.

at shortshop and Gordy Coleman at first base. Coleman had come to Cincinnati from Cleveland along with pitcher Cal McLish and second baseman Billy Martin in exchange for Johnny Temple. Martin played just one year for the Reds (between 1957 and 1961, Billy played for seven different teams, an apparent warmup for his managerial career). Martin's most notable hit that year came off the jaw of Cubs reliever Jim Brewer, after Billy stalked out to the mound to discuss a high inside pitch. The blow broke a bone in Brewer's face, the pitcher sued, and when the whole business was settled Billy was minus a reported $25,000 in damages.

The Reds finished sixth in 1960, but Hutchinson was convinced the team was better than that, and a year later would prove it. (The best thing to happen to the Reds that summer went virtually unnoticed, except in a certain local household. On June 5, 1960, the Reds signed nineteen-year-old infielder Pete Rose, star of Cincinnati's Western Hills High School team. With a $7,000 bonus in the bank, Pete went off to the team's Geneva, New York, farm club.)

Expansion was coming to the National League, which had voted to enroll two new members in 1962, enlarging the league to 10 teams (which the American League was planning to do in 1961). The two new franchises would be New York and Houston, and it was to take over the latter that Gabe Paul brought to an end his long association with the Cincinnati Reds. Replacing Paul was Bill De-Witt, a man with a long history of front-office service. In the 1930s, Bill and his brother Charlie had owned the St. Louis Browns, selling the franchise to Bill Veeck in 1951. He later served as assistant general manager of the New York Yankees and president of the Detroit Tigers.

One of DeWitt's first moves was to get rid of Billy Martin, selling him to Milwaukee. Then, in a three-way transaction, the Reds swapped Roy McMillan to the Braves for right-hander Joey Jay and left-hander Juan Pizarro, immediately shipping Pizarro and Cal McLish to the White Sox for third baseman Gene Freese. Early in the season, DeWitt filled the second-base hole by trading for Giants keystone man Don Blasingame, sending San Francisco catcher Ed Bailey.

Hutchinson's infield was Coleman at first, Blasingame at second, Eddie Kasko at short, and Freese at third. The outfield was Robinson, Pinson, Bell, Lynch, and Post (reacquired from the Phillies). The catching was in the hands of two offensively weak but defensively strong receivers: Jerry Zimmerman and Johnny Edwards.

Joey Jay (1961–1966), a 21-game winner in 1961 and again in 1962.

Hutchinson's frontline starters were Jay, O'Toole, and Purkey, with Brosnan and left-hander Billy Henry in the pen.

The preseason poll of 232 members of the Baseball Writers Association conducted by *The Sporting News* found not a single writer predicting a Cincinnati pennant.

Sadly, Powel Crosley did not live long enough to share in all the excitement of 1961. The Reds' long-time owner died at the age of seventy-four, on March 28. Ownership of the team passed to the Crosley family, and it soon became apparent that the Reds would be put up for sale before long.

The Reds started poorly in 1961, posting a 6–10 record in April, but then tearing loose and running up the best one-month record of any team in the league that season—20–6. They followed this with a 19–12 June and an 18–12 July. By this time the rest of the league knew that this Cincinnati outfit was genuine.

The Reds had to fight off a tenacious Los Angeles Dodgers team, with a critical moment coming in a doubleheader in L.A. on August 16. With first place at stake, Purkey and O'Toole delivered 6–0 and 8–0 shutouts. This allowed the Reds to take possession of the penthouse, and although it was a precarious position at times, they were not to be dislodged. On September 26, Cincinnati clinched its fourth pennant and first in 21 years.

Gene Freese (1961–1963), third baseman on the 1961 pennant winners.

The big man was Frank Robinson, hammering 37 home runs, amassing 124 RBIs, batting .323, and compiling a league-high slugging mark of .611, all of which earned him the MVP Award that fall.

Right there with Robinson was Vada Pinson, batting a career-high .343 and leading the league with 208 hits. Gordy Coleman provided some punch at first base with 26 homers, while Gene Freese delivered the sock the club had hoped for, 26 homers and 87 RBIs. Playing part time, Post belted 20 homers and batted .294. The Reds also had a potent weapon in pinch-hitter Jerry Lynch. The hard-hitting outfielder, who batted .315 in ninety-six games, was lethal in the pinch, going 19 for 47 (.404). Lynch, whose 19 pinch hits had lead the league in 1960, again had the most hits for any substitute swinger.

This time a tough-swinging Cincinnati club had the pitching to make the runs count. Jay became the club's first twenty-game winner since Blackwell in 1947, going 21–10. O'Toole was 19–9, and Purkey, 16–12. Brosnan headed up the bullpen, winning 10

Don Blasingame (1961–1963) had the second base job locked up . . . but along came Rose.

Johnny Edwards (1961–1967), his lifetime .992 fielding average is the highest of any catcher in National League history.

Bill Henry (1960–1965), Cincinnati's hard-throwing relief specialist.

Two-thirds of anybody's outfield: Vada Pinson *(left)* and Frank Robinson. In 1961 Pinson batted .343 and Robinson, .323.

Bob Purkey (1958–1964), who gave the Reds a sensational 23–5 record in 1962.

Outfielder Marty Keough (1962–1965).

and saving 16. (These saves were computed retroactively; the save did not become an officially designated statistic until 1966.) Righthander Ken Johnson, picked up from Kansas City in late July, helped with a 6–2 record.

Unfortunately for the Reds, their World Series terrain was a loaded minefield. As their forebears of 1939 had, this Reds club had to do combat with an awesomely powerful Yankee combine. In winning 109 games, Ralph Houk's 1961 Yankees had blasted a record shattering 240 home runs, led by Roger Maris's monumental 61, Mickey Mantle's 54, and so on to lesser but still troublesome totals by Bill Skowron, Yogi Berra, Elston Howard,

Crosley Field in the early 1960s.

Joey Jay at work against the Yankees in his winning effort in Game 2 of the 1961 World Series.

and Johnny Blanchard. In addition to these heavy pounders, the club had a snappy keystone combination in second baseman Bobby Richardson and shortstop Tony Kubek and a defensive wizard in third baseman Clete Boyer. The Yankee pitching featured ace left-hander Whitey Ford and right-handers Ralph Terry and Bill Stafford.

There seemed no way the Reds could win this Series, nor did they. In the opener at Yankee Stadium, the Reds went down 2–0 to Ford's 2-hitter, O'Toole pitching well in a losing cause. The Reds won their only game of the Series behind Jay the next day, 6–2.

The Series began slipping away from the Reds in the late innings of Game 3, at Crosley Field. Leading 2–1 behind Purkey after seven, the Reds lost to solo home runs by Blanchard (pinch hit) and Maris in the eighth and ninth. After that it was all New York.

Game 4 went to Ford and the Yankees, 7–0, over O'Toole. Before being forced to leave in the sixth inning because of an injury, Ford had set a new World Series record for consecutive shutout innings, 32, snapping the long-standing record established by Red Sox left-hander Babe Ruth during the World War I era. (Ruth had delivered 29.2 straight World Series goose egg innings.)

In Game 5, the Yankees disposed of Jay with a 5-run first inning and went on from there to a 13–5 world championship victory.

For Reds fans, however, the gloom of a World Series defeat could not sour the sweet taste of an unexpected pennant. (There would be a nine-year wait for their next flag, which by then-existing Cincinnati standards was right around the corner.)

Hutchinson's club came roaring back in 1962 to win 98 games, a new record high for the franchise and more than enough to win most years (44 National League pennants had, in fact, been won with as many or fewer wins), but in 1962, 98 meant no better than third place. It was the year when the Giants and Dodgers deadlocked at the end of the season with identical 101–61 records. (Pittsburgh set a record for a fourth-place team with 93 victories. These rather lush victory totals for so many teams were in large part subsidized by the 120 defeats suffered by the expansion New York Mets, then part of the league's new 10-team structure.)

The club was now under the charge of Bill DeWitt, who headed a new corporation that had on March 23, 1962, consummated the transaction in which the Powel Crosley Foundation transferred ownership for $4,625,000.

Things began poorly for the Reds in the spring, when Freese suffered an ankle fracture that disabled him for virtually the entire season (he was never the same player after the injury). Juggling his infield, Hutchinson moved Kasko to third and installed Leo Cardenas at short.

The Reds hit with some authority in 1962, with Robinson improving on his MVP year: .342 average, 39 home runs, 136 RBIs, 208 hits, and league-leading figures in slugging (.624) and doubles (51). Pinson fell to .292 but drove in 100 runs, while Coleman poled 28 homers.

For the first time since the Walters-Derringer glory days, the club put up a pair

A restless Fred Hutchinson pacing the dugout.

Outfielder Tommy Harper (1962–1967), his 126 runs led the league in 1965.

of twenty-game winners in Purkey (23–5) and Jay (21–14). O'Toole was 16–13. Young Jim Maloney moved into the anteroom of stardom with a 9–7 record, blazing his fastball for 105 strikeouts in 115 innings. A familiar face made yet another reappearance in Cincinnati. After the 1960 season, Joe Nuxhall had been traded to Kansas City, pitched briefly for California and then gone to the minors, from where the Reds hauled him up in late July. The big left-hander rewarded the faith by posting a 5–0 record over the rest of the season.

When the Reds went to spring training in 1963 they considered themselves set at second base, where thirty-year-old Don Blasingame was the regular. Blasingame had turned in one of his better seasons in 1962, batting .281 and fielding well. But charging into camp that spring was a rookie second baseman of seemingly inexhaustible drive and hustle. He was a switch-hitter, he ran out ground balls and pop flies and even bases on balls at top speed. He performed with a flooding abundance of spirit and desire, and his style of play caught the eye and turned heads and brought smiles of recognition. Twenty-two-year-old Pete Rose had arrived.

On opening day, the Cincinnati native, who had come to camp as a nonroster player and been given little chance of unseating Blasingame, was the starting second baseman. On April 13, 1963, after 12 hitless at bats, Rose rifled a triple off of Pittsburgh's Bob Friend, picking up the first of what two decades later would have been built into the largest hit collection in baseball history.

The team finished fifth in 1963. Pinson (.313) was the only .300 hitter on the squad, lining out a league-high 204 hits and 14 triples. Rose, voted Rookie of the Year, broke

Jim Maloney (1960–1970). Nobody threw harder.

in with a .273 average. Purkey and Jay, the big winners of the year before, faltered badly, Purkey falling to 6–10 and Jay, to 7–18. O'Toole was 17–14 and Nuxhall, 15–8, but the ace was Maloney, who flashed to stardom with a 23–7 record, 6 shutouts, and 265 strikeouts (but like every other pitcher in the league, was overshadowed in all departments by the Dodgers' Sandy Koufax). On May 21, 1963, Maloney tied Noodles Hahn's sixty-two-year-old club record when he fanned 16 Milwaukee Braves batters in one game.

The following year, 1964, began ominously for the Reds. Early in January it was announced that Hutchinson was suffering from chest cancer. After undergoing two months of radiology treatment, the skipper proclaimed that he was "clean" and plunged into spring training. It soon became obvious, however, that Hutch was far from clean. Tough, stubborn, and proud, Hutchinson fought the agony of spreading cancer with painkillers, never complaining, insisting he was fine, even when the evidence was plainly to the contrary. By mid-July, he stopped making road trips and turned the club over to coach Dick Sisler.

Late in the 1964 season the Reds suddenly and unexpectedly found themselves in a pennant race. Gene Mauch's Phillies had been cruising at the top when to the astonishment of everyone, the Philadelphia world began to come apart.

When the Reds departed for an eastern trip to New York and Philadelphia on September 21, they were 6½ games behind with 13 to play. It was like a trip to "Fantasy Island": They won 8 straight and when they returned home were in first place. At this point, with the Phillies continuing to lose, the Cardinals also entered the race and it became a three-team scramble between the surging Reds and Cardinals and the demoralized Phillies, who lost 10 straight before arching their backs and inflicting some fatal damage on the Reds.

On the final day of the season the Reds and

Rookie Pete Rose (1963–1978, 1984–1986).

Cardinals were tied for first place, the Phillies—playing in Cincinnati—were one game behind. While the Cardinals were winning in New York, the aroused Phillies drew some bitter satisfaction from the dregs of their soured season by eliminating the Reds with a 10–0 drubbing.

Some better stickwork might have won it for the Reds in 1964—their .249 club batting average was seventh best in the league, with only Robinson (.306) hitting over .300. Some unexpected help came from first baseman Deron Johnson, who hit 21 home runs, but Pinson fell to .266. O'Toole led the staff with a

John Tsitouris, who started and relieved for the Reds between 1962 and 1968.

17–7 record, Maloney slipping from his big season to 15–10.

On April 23, 1964, the Reds had won one of baseball's memorable games. Houston's Ken Johnson (formerly with the Reds) was locked in a scoreless duel with Nuxhall, with Johnson working on a no-hitter going into the top of the ninth. In that inning Rose bunted to the mound, where Johnson fielded it cleanly but threw wildly to first, enabling Rose to go to second. Pete went to third on a ground out, then scored on an infield error. When Nuxhall retired Houston in the bottom of the ninth, the Reds had a 1–0 victory and Johnson had the doubtful distinction of having lost a no-hitter.

Soon after the season, on October 19, 1964, the critically ill Hutchinson resigned. His successor was Dick Sisler, who had run the team through much of the season's second half. On November 12, Hutchinson died in Bradenton, Florida, at the age of forty-five.

"He was one of those big, tough, gruff guys that everybody liked," one Cincinnati writer said of the late skipper. "He had a positive impact on a lot of his players. Many of them realized it and appreciated it and will remember him fondly for the rest of their lives."

Southpaw Billy McCool (1964–1968), a reliever with plenty of smoke, had 120 strikeouts in 105 innings in 1965.

T·H·I·R·T·E·E·N

GETTING READY FOR TAKEOFF

THE building of the greatest team in their history and quite possibly in National League history as well, was done quietly and methodically by the Reds, the supporting pillars being placed with an emphasis on strength and longevity. Rose was the first, and in 1965 he was joined by Tony Perez.

The twenty-three-year-old Perez (who came up as a first baseman, then was switched to third for five years) was one of the most popular players ever to wear a Reds uniform, among fans and teammates alike. Always smiling, always congenial, he was a soothing clubhouse presence. He was to become regarded as the toughest clutch hitter on a team of superstars, absolutely deadly with men on base, with eleven straight years of 90 or more RBIs to prove it.

Tony Perez (1964–1976, 1984–1986), one of the most respected of all Cincinnati players.

Tony broke in modestly in 1965, getting into 104 games and batting .260 on a team that finished fourth despite a trio of .300 hitters, the RBI leader, the hits leader, and two twenty-game winners.

Managed by Sisler, the Reds had a solid 89–73 record, but wound up eight games behind the first-place Dodgers. Coleman batted .302; Rose, .312; and Pinson, .305. Rose led with 209 hits (the first of what was going to be a record-breaking 10 seasons of more than 200 hits). Deron Johnson, playing third base that year, led with 130 RBIs and hit 32 home runs, and Frank Robinson hit 33 crowd pleasers and knocked in 113 runs. The team as a whole batted .273, the league's best and 28 points higher than the Dodgers, and scored the most runs, 825, an incredible 217 more than the pennant winners. The difference between the two clubs was named Koufax and Drysdale, winners of 49 games between them.

Cincinnati's pitching was crested by right-hander Sammy Ellis (22–10) and Maloney (20–9). Nuxhall was 11–4 and southpaw

Dick Sisler, who managed the Reds in 1964 and 1965. He played briefly for the team in 1952.

Deron Johnson (1964–1967) played first, third, and outfield for the Reds. In 1965 he had 32 home runs and a league-leading 130 RBIs.

Sammy Ellis (1962, 1964–1967), a 22-game winner in 1965.

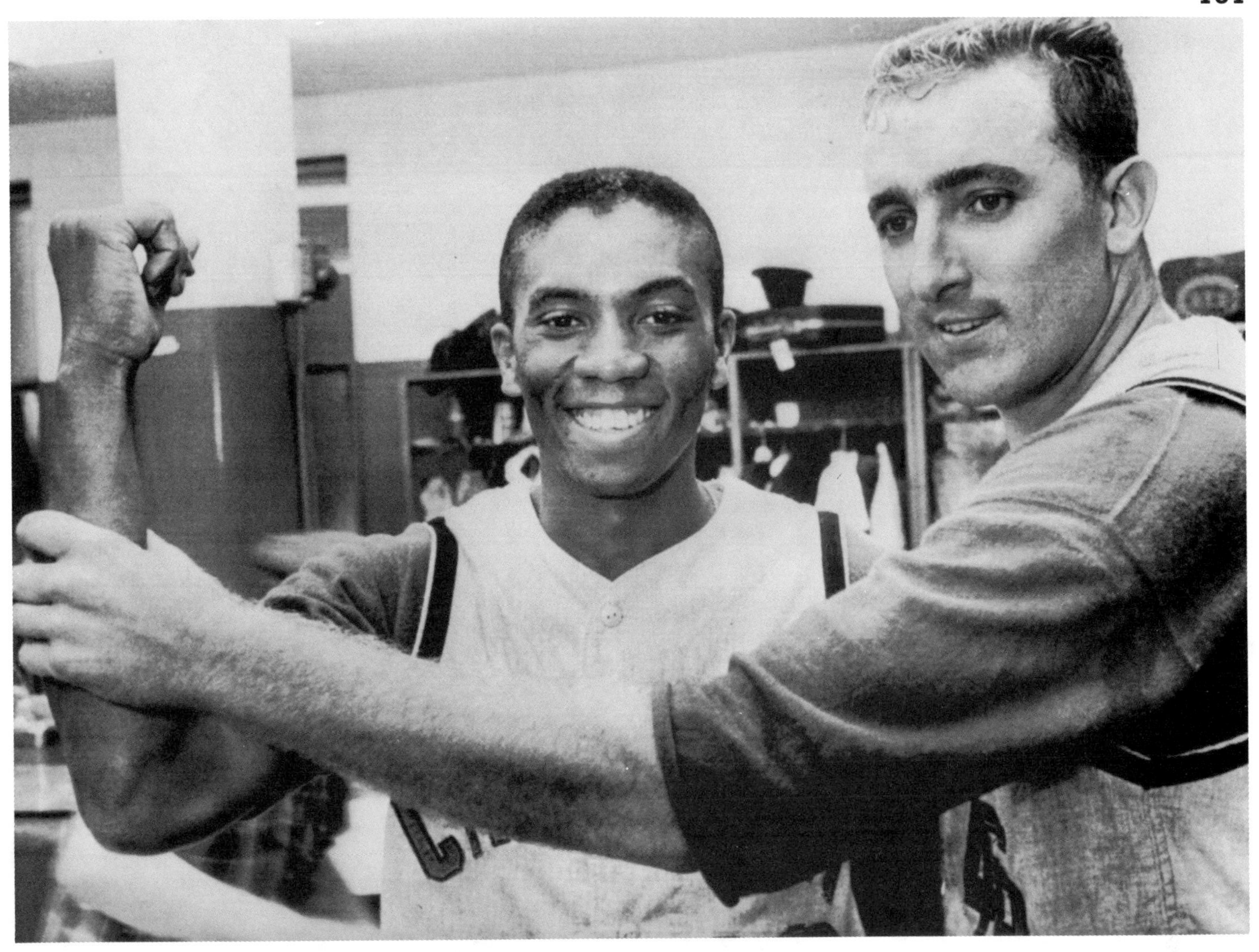

Chico Cardenas *(left)* has just won a ten-inning, 1–0 no-hitter for Jim Maloney with a home run. Maloney is feeling the forearm muscle that smote the blow. Maloney pitched his gem on August 19, 1965.

Billy McCool provided strong relief, but the Reds' ERA was 3.89 to the Dodgers' 2.81, and therein lay the gap between first and fourth places.

Koufax and Maloney were the toughest pitchers in the league to hit, with the Cincinnati fastballer turning in a handful of gems. On April 19, he one-hit the Braves. On June 14 he pitched 10 hitless innings against the Mets, gave up a home run to Johnny Lewis in the eleventh and lost 1–0, surrendering just that 1 hit, 1 walk, and striking out 18. On August 19, he again pitched 10 hitless innings, against the Cubs, this time winning 1–0 on Leo Cardenas's home run in the top of the tenth.

On June 8, 1965, baseball held its first amateur free-agent draft. Cincinnati's top pick was outfielder Bernie Carbo, who proved to be an excellent choice. But with their second pick they broke the bank, selecting seventeen-year-old catcher Johnny Bench from a bump in the road called Binger, Oklahoma.

What the Cincinnati organization had

Mr. Johnny Lee Bench, selected by the Reds in the June 1965 free-agent draft. Here he is with Peninsula of the Carolina League in 1966.

heard about the boy was this: He had enormous hands, capable of holding seven baseballs in one hand; the strength of his throwing arm had to be seen to be believed; he could hit a baseball out of sight; his maturity and professionalism were remarkable for a seventeen-year-old.

Frank Robinson: They said he was "an old thirty." Well, he wasn't.

"He seemed like a good choice," a Reds scout said dryly, years later.

So on June 8 the Reds had made a felicitous decision; after the season, on December 9, 1965, they made a disastrous one. On that day, DeWitt traded Frank Robinson to the Baltimore Orioles for pitchers Milt Pappas and Jack Baldschun and outfielder Dick Simpson, with Pappas the key man for the Reds.

Explaining the move, which stunned many a front office, DeWitt used a rationale which was to come back to haunt him: although Robinson was only thirty years old, DeWitt said he believed that Frank "was an old thirty." (The comment never failed to rankle the proud and fiercely competitive Robinson; he even alluded to it in his Hall of Fame induction speech in 1983.) Robinson went on to become a Triple Crown winner, MVP, and the galvanizing force behind three Baltimore pennant winners, while Pappas delivered what he had always delivered—workmanlike, but unspectacular, pitching.

Milt Pappas (1966–1968), remembered principally in Cincinnati as the man who was traded for Frank Robinson. Don't blame Milt.

Dave Bristol, who managed the Reds from 1966 to 1969.

When they took the field for the start of the 1966 season, the Reds had a new manager. Sisler had been fired the previous October and replaced by Don Heffner. Heffner was a mild-mannered former American League second baseman who had played for the Browns when DeWitt was running that franchise. Despite a dozen years as a minor-league manager, Heffner lacked the touch to bring the Reds together as a unit and, recognizing his mistake, DeWitt was forced to let his friend go in midseason. On July 13, Heffner was replaced by one of his coaches, Dave Bristol. The thirty-three-year-old Bristol, who had never played in the majors, was a more aggressive personality than Heffner and was always a highly regarded baseball man (he later managed at Milwaukee, Atlanta, and San Francisco).

In eighth place when Bristol took over, the

Third baseman Tommy Helms, National League Rookie of the Year in 1966, was with the Reds from 1964 to 1971.

club perked up slightly for the new man, but at the end could do no better than seventh. Rose, now an established star, did the best hitting with a .313 average and 205 hits. First baseman Lee May, soon to become known as "The Big Bopper," appeared in twenty-five games at the end of the season, bopped the first two of his 354 career homers and batted .333. Maloney was 16–8, Ellis fell to 12–19, Pappas was 12–11, and McCool continued strong out of the pen, saving 18 games. The club produced its third Rookie of the Year in third baseman Tommy Helms, a .284 hitter.

On December 5, 1966, ownership of the Cincinnati Reds once again changed hands. A group led by Francis Dale, publisher of the *Cincinnati Enquirer,* bought out the DeWitt interests for around $7 million. Dale became president of the club and on January 22, 1967 announced the selection of Bob Howsam as general manager.

A former minor-league club owner, Howsam had left baseball and gone into the investment business, in which he was occupied in August 1964 when the Cardinals asked him to take over their front office. This was the year when a Cardinal surge combined with a Phillies collapse to bring St. Louis a dramatic last-minute pennant. Along the way, Howsam earned some good notices and a lot of recognition. When Dale offered him a three-year contract, Howsam accepted,

Outfielder Art Shamky (1965–1967) had 21 homers in 234 at bats in 1966.

bringing Dick Wagner along with him as his assistant.

In his first full season as manager, Dave Bristol brought the team home forth, winning a respectable 87 games. The Reds had become a bit crowded by their own talent. With Lee May taking over at first base, Perez was moved to third, forcing Helms to second and Rose to the outfield (the first of several position moves this compliant superstar willingly agreed to). Perez was the team's top gunner with 26 home runs and 102 RBIs, with Rose the high man with a .301 average.

The star of the 1967 pitching staff was nineteen-year-old fireballing Gary Nolan, breaking in with a 14–8 record and 206 strikeouts. Pappas was 16–13 and Maloney, 15–11. Still firing one of baseball's imperial fastballs, Maloney on August 16 retired the first nineteen Pittsburgh batters he faced, then injured his ankle and had to leave the game. (McCool allowed two hits in completing a 4–0 victory.) Submarine-balling right-hander Ted Abernathy gave the Reds some of the best relief pitching they'd ever had: 70 games, 28 saves, 63 hits in 106 innings, 1.27 ERA.

There was no way of knowing at the time, of course, but August 28, 1967 was a nota-

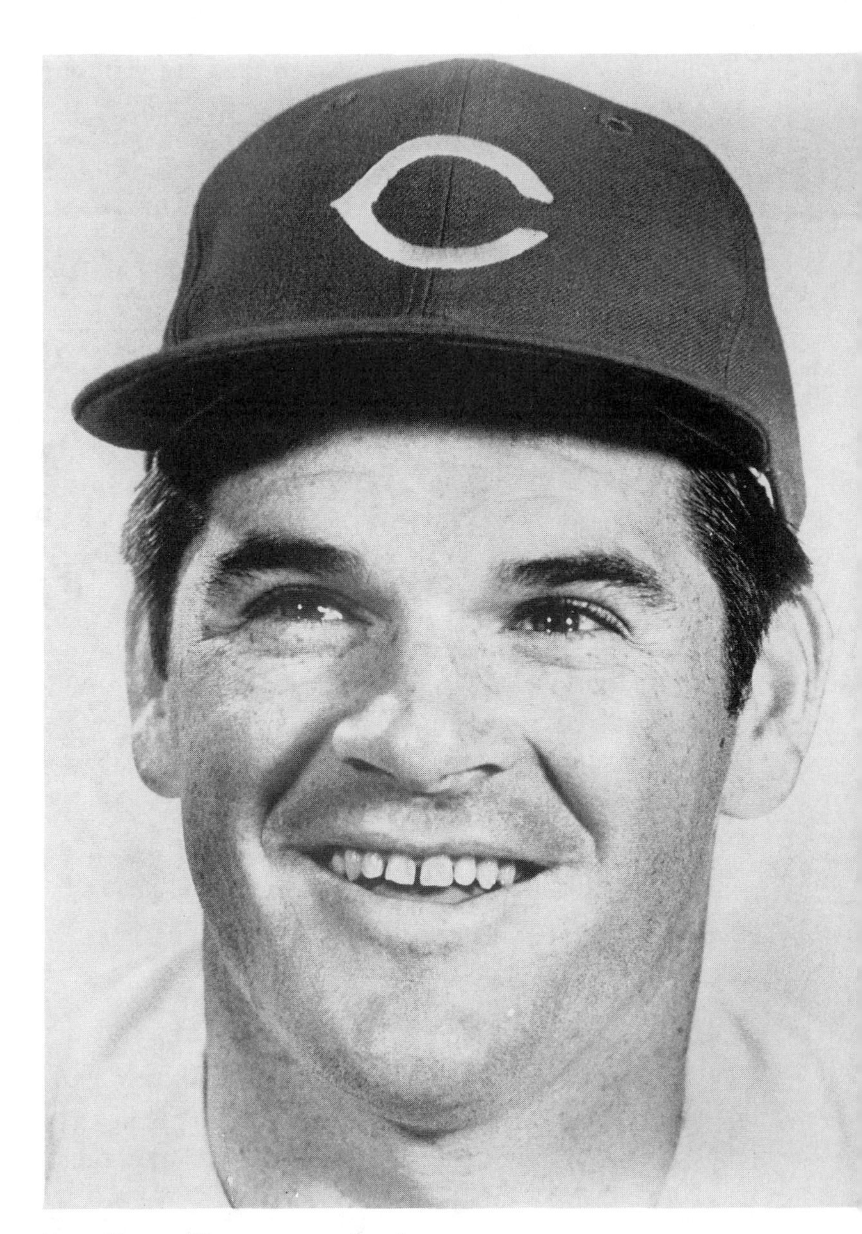

Pete Rose: Those were the days.

Backup catcher Don Pavletich (1957, 1959, 1962–1968). He also filled in at first base.

Gary Nolan (1967–1973, 1975–1977) was a star at nineteen, only to have injuries ruin what promised to be a great career.

tion date for baseball's historical calendar, especially if you were a Cincinnati Reds fan. That was the day that nineteen-year-old Johnny Bench made his debut behind the plate for the Reds. Johnny's sense of the dramatic, which he was to demonstrate on many later occasions, was not present that day—he went 0 for 3 and was pinch-hit for in the ninth inning. The youngster got into nineteen games, hit one home run and batted .163. The hazy beginning was deemed irrelevant; the boy was so obviously an exemplar of stardom, with his most prominent quality his arm.

"He throws like nobody I've ever seen," one veteran scout said, "and I've seen everybody."

"When Johnny Bench throws," one executive said, "everybody in baseball drools."

And there were some who maintained that Bench could throw as hard as Nolan Ryan.

Bench had arrived just in time for a bit of history. On September 1, three days after his debut, the Reds played the longest game in

Ted Abernathy (1967–1968), who gave the Reds two years of superb relief work, leading the league in appearances in each of his years with the Reds.

Johnny Bench (1967–1983), Cincinnati's two-time MVP and Hall-of-Fame catcher.

their history, a 21-inning, 1–0 loss to the Giants at Crosley Field.

Even as the Reds were putting together their greatest ball club, they were building a more appropriate display case for it: on February 1, 1968, ground was broken and work on Riverfront Stadium begun.

Bench became the club's fourth Rookie of the Year in 1968, narrowly edging out New York Mets left-hander Jerry Koosman. Johnny set a rookie record for catchers by appearing with mask and mitt in 154 games, the first of 13 consecutive years of catching 100 or more games (a major-league record he shares with Yankee catcher Bill Dickey). Bench batted .275 in his maiden voyage around the league, with 15 home runs. Significantly, he led all catchers in assists, shooting down 102 baserunners, most by a National League catcher since 1936. (It was the only year Bench ever led in assists, and the explanation was simple: They all but stopped running on him.)

The Reds finished fourth in 1968, but hit hard, leading the league in batting (.273), slugging (.389), runs (690), and doubles (281, which set a new team record). This was impressive that year, for 1968 was the "Year of the Pitcher," when the league batted .243 overall.

Right-hander George Culver (1968–1969). One of his 11 wins in 1968 was a no-hitter.

The tight pitching, however, did not extend to the Cincinnati staff, which logged a 3.56 ERA, the worst in the league. Maloney was 16–10 and lefty Jerry Arrigo 12–10. Nolan, beginning to suffer the arm miseries that were to bedevil and then finally abort his career, was 9–4. Right-hander George Culver was 11–16, with one memorable day—on July 29 he no-hit the Phillies, winning 6–1.

On June 11, 1968, the Reds bit the bullet on the disastrous Frank Robinson deal by trading Pappas and two lesser lights to the Braves for right-handers Tony Cloninger and Clay Carroll, and infielder Woody Woodward (later to become the club's assistant general manager). Carroll was soon to become one of the great relievers in Reds history.

One man who overcame the Year of the Pitcher was Pete Rose, who edged out Pittsburgh's Matty Alou on the last day of the season to win the batting championship, .335 to .332. The day before, Rose, who had 210 hits for the season, had gone 5 for 5, positioning himself to win his first title and the seventh in Cincinnati history.

Soon after the close of the season, Howsam traded long-time star Vada Pinson to the Cardinals for outfielder Bobby Tolan and slim right-handed reliever Wayne Granger. After a decade of playing regularly in the Reds outfield, the thirty-two-year-old Pinson had begun to slide. Vada had given the club some stellar seasons, but had never quite attained the level of stardom his many talents had promised.

A few weeks later, another veteran of the 1960s, shortstop Leo Cardenas, was traded to the Minnesota Twins for left-hander Jim Merritt.

The major leagues expanded to 12 teams each in 1969, and this resulted in what for the conservative baseball establishment was a radical new structuring: 6-team, East and West divisions, with the division winners playing each other in a postseason series to determine the league champion. (The playoff series was then a best-of-5 shootout; the current 7-game format was not instituted until 1985.) The new National League clubs were Montreal and San Diego.

Posted in the Western Division in the new alignment, the Reds began divisional play as a third-place club, finishing four games behind Atlanta. Once again, the Reds hit well, leading in home runs (171), slugging (.422), and runs (798).

Lee May blasted 38 homers and had 110 RBIs and Tony Perez (a third baseman then) hit 37 long ones and had 122 RBIs. Tolan hit for a .305 mark, and outfielder Alex Johnson

First baseman Lee May (1965–1971), was called "The Big Bopper," and in 1969 he bopped 38 of them.

Utility infielder Chico Ruiz (1964–1969).

was at .315. The club's most consistent puncher was again Rose, with 218 hits and, with a .348 average, a second straight batting title. For Pete, it was a repeat performance in more ways than one. In 1968 he had nosed past Pirate outfielder Matty Alou on the season's last day; in 1969 he did the same to another Pittsburgh outfielder—the great Roberto Clemente—and won the crown by three points.

A shortstop tandem of Woody Woodward and Darrel Chaney had not adequately replaced Cardenas, but the club had high hopes for a youngster about to be promoted from the minors, Dave Concepcion.

Merritt led a shaky staff with 17–9, and Maloney was 12–5. For the twenty-nine-year-old Maloney, this was to be his last full year in a Reds uniform. Shoulder problems and a torn Achilles tendon suffered the following spring were to spell the end of what should have been one of pitching's glittering careers. Before his candle sputtered out, however, Maloney fired his third no-hitter (including the ten-inning effort he lost), rolling over Houston, 10–0, at Crosley Field on April 30, 1969. (The next day, Houston's Don Wilson returned the favor by no-hitting the Reds.) In addition to his array of no-hitters, the exceptionally hard-throwing Maloney also delivered five career 1-hitters. Also that year, reliever Wayne Granger set a club record by answering 90 calls from the bullpen.

At the conclusion of the season, on October 8, 1969, Dave Bristol was fired. The new manager was hired the next day. Together, he and the Cincinnati Reds prepared to head into the new decade, which would prove to be the most successful in the long history of America's oldest professional baseball team.

F·O·U·R·T·E·E·N

SPARKY AND THE INFERNAL MACHINE

GEORGE Lee Anderson spent his first six years in professional baseball (1953–1958) as an infielder—mostly a second baseman—in the Brooklyn Dodgers organization. Not a power hitter, he hit for respectable averages and showed range and hustle in the field by frequently leading his various leagues in putouts and assists.

After the 1958 season, the Dodgers traded Anderson to the Philadelphia Phillies, and in 1959 he spent his first and only season as a major-league player, batting .218, hitting no home runs, playing a good second base, and impressing people with his keen, baseball-wise judgment.

He spent the next four years playing second base for Toronto, then in the International League, hitting modestly, fielding well, and taking what was in effect a managerial interest in everything that went on around him.

Eddie Sawyer, the Phillies' manager when Anderson played his one year in the big leagues, said, "It was obvious to me and a lot of other people that George Anderson was managerial timber. He understood the game, he was a fine judge of talent, and he had the gift of getting along with people, which may be the most important part of successful managing."

That managerial career began with Toronto in 1964, when Anderson—already known by the nickname that was to become one of the most famous in sports—was just thirty years old. He later managed four other clubs and had just signed as a coach with the

A rather somber Sparky Anderson *(left)* is being introduced to the Cincinnati press corps as the Reds new manager by Bob Howsam. The date is October 9, 1969.

California Angels when Howsam offered him the big job at Cincinnati.

Sparky's first year, 1970, produced a big winner as his club ran off with the division title. Winning 50 of their first 70 games, the Reds (first known that year as "The Big Red Machine"), were out of first place for only one day all season, won the division over the

Johnny Bench. Cincinnati was a 17-year interlude between Binger, Oklahoma, and Cooperstown, New York.

Dodgers by 14 1/2 games, and set a new club attendance record of 1,803,568, as well as a new peak in victories with a 102–60 ledger.

In winning their first pennant in nine years, the Reds enjoyed a good blend of heavy hitting and strong pitching, with The Machine gunners leading the league in home runs (191), batting (.270), and slugging (.436). No less than 119 of the homers were hit by three men—Bench (45, most in the league), Perez (40), and May (34). Bench, who was the league's MVP that year, also led the league with 148 runs batted in, while Perez had 129.

Augmenting these long-range bombers were Tolan, who batted .316 and led the league with 57 stolen bases; rookie outfielder Bernie Carbo (.310), and Rose, who had a league-leading 205 hits, .316 batting average, and—with a $105,000 salary—the distinction of becoming the club's first six-figure player. (Twenty years later, Pete's landmark salary would approximate the major-league minimum.) In addition, the team had sealed up the gap at shortstop for the better part of the next two decades. The new man was a tall and slender Venezuelan, Dave Concepcion, launching a 19-year career, the longest uninterrupted skein in franchise history.

Making sure that this lavish offense was not wasted was a pitching staff that was deep and capable, as well as somewhat snake bit.

Tony Perez.

Outfielder Bobby Tolan (1969–1970, 1972–1973) led the league with 57 stolen bases in 1970.

Outfielder Bernie Carbo (1969–1972) batted .310 in his rookie year.

Dave Concepcion (1970–1988), who played 2,165 games at shortstop for the Reds.

Jim Merritt turned in a 20–12 record before hurting his elbow on August 26, an injury that all but wrecked his career. A hulking rookie right-hander, twenty-one-year-old Wayne Simpson, won his first ten decisions and had a 13–1 record when he tore a muscle in his right shoulder on July 31. With the injury went Simpson's fastball (which they said had to be measured by the science of ballistics) and a career that had begun with boundless promise. (Simpson labored through five more seasons, with three clubs other than Cincinnati, but what was lost on July 31, 1970, never came back.)

Making a comeback from his own ailments was Garry Nolan, racking up an 18–7 record. Right-hander Jim McGlothlin, acquired from California in the off-season, broke out to an 11–4 record but then was hit twice by line drives and was never the same, ending with a 14–10 mark. (It was hard luck to the end of the line for Jim; he died of cancer in 1975 at the age of forty-two.)

Jim Merritt (1969–1972), who was a twenty-game winner in 1970.

Blessed with a bullpen that was going to get better and better as the decade lengthened, Sparky in 1970 had Granger (35 saves), Carroll, and a nineteen-year-old left-hander named Don Gullett (also to have an injury-scarred career) with a dynamite fastball. Together, the relief corps posted 60 saves, a league record that the staff tied in 1972.

Adding to the summer-long festivity that was the 1970 baseball season in the city of Cincinnati was the opening of the team's new home, Riverfront Stadium. The Reds played their final game at Crosley Field, their home grounds for 58 years, on June 24, then moved on to Riverfront, built at a reported cost of $48 million.

Right-hander Jim McGlothlin (1970–1973), a 14-game winner in 1970.

Right-hander Wayne Simpson (1970–1972), who was overpowering until he injured his shoulder.

Located on a forty-eight acre site near downtown Cincinnati, Riverfront opened at a particularly auspicious time in Reds history, for the club was about to tear through its most successful decade and the commodious new park (more than 50,000 seats) enabled throngs of heartland Reds fans to come streaming from all directions to thrill to the might and power of The Big Red Machine and send franchise attendance records soaring. (The only drawback to the new park was, in the opinion of many, that anathema of modern baseball, the artificial surface.)

A few weeks after its opening, Riverfront was the scene of the 1970 All-Star Game. It was in this game that Pete Rose scored what

Wayne Granger (1969–1971), Cincinnati's tireless reliever, who set a club record with 90 appearances in 1969.

Riverfront Stadium.

is probably the most celebrated run of his long career, when he knocked catcher Ray Fosse senseless in scoring the winning run in the bottom of the twelfth inning in the National League's 5–4 win.

In a pennant playoff series for the first time, Sparky's boys never broke stride, sweeping the Eastern Division champion Pirates in three straight. Nolan, with relief help from Carroll, won the opener, 3–0, in ten innings. The second game saw Merritt, Carroll, and Gullett combine for a 3–1 win. The sweep was completed at Riverfront in another tightly pitched game. Home runs by Perez and Bench gave the Reds a 2–1 lead in the bottom of the first, and a Tolan base hit in the bottom of the eighth broke a 2–2 tie and gave the Reds a 3–2 pennant-winning victory. Sparky employed four pitchers in this one, with Granger and Gullett closing the lid in the ninth.

The 1970 World Series was a matchup between two truly outstanding clubs. Earl Weaver's Baltimore Orioles had won an impressive 108 games and had a staff of four twenty-game winners (only the second time in the century this had happened) in Jim Palmer, Dave McNally, Mike Cuellar, and Pat Dobson. Also on hand were power-hitting first baseman Boog Powell, second baseman Dave Johnson (later the manager of the New York Mets), the magic-gloved Mark Belanger at short, and the equally brilliant Brooks Robinson at third. Another defensive wizard, Paul Blair, was in center, hustling Don Buford in right, and in left was Cincinnati's one-time star Frank Robinson. Elrod Hendricks and Andy Etchebarren divided the catching.

Led by the scintillating play of Robinson at third base, this Baltimore squad proved to be an irresistible tide. They took the first two games at Riverfront by scores of 4–3 and 6–5, beating Nolan and rookie reliever Milt Wilcox. Game 3 was an Oriole runaway, 9–3, with Tony Cloninger losing.

The Reds won their only game of the Series the next day, 6–5, thanks to a three-run

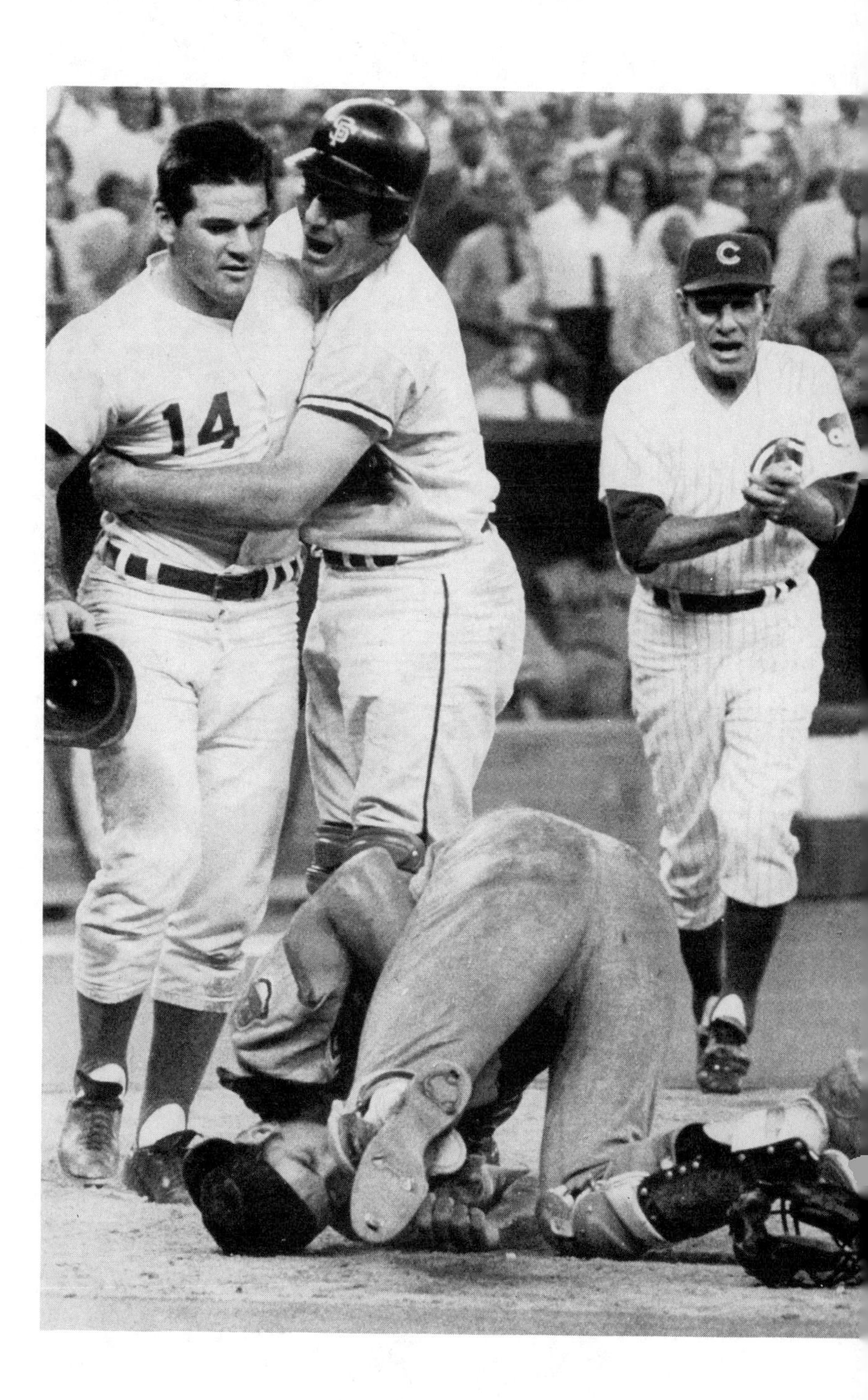

Pete Rose has just bowled over catcher Ray Fosse to win the 1970 All-Star Game for the National League at Riverfront. The Giants Dick Dietz is congratulating Pete while an elated Leo Durocher applauds. Everybody seems delighted except Fosse.

A bit of action from the 1970 World Series. It's the top of the seventh inning of Game 2 and Cincinnati shortstop Woody Woodward has just forced Baltimore's Paul Blair at second and has fired on to first to double up Boog Powell. Woodward played short for the Reds from 1968 to 1971.

eighth-inning home run by May, Carroll getting the win. But Baltimore took it all home in Game 5 with another 9–3 win, pounding away at Merritt and five other pitchers after the Reds had scored all their runs in the top of the first.

Baltimore's pitching held the Reds to a .213 average, with only May and young outfielder Hal McRae doing any sustained hitting. The Orioles, on the other hand, hit Sparky's pitchers freely, averaging .292 for the five games and hitting 10 home runs.

Nevertheless, the Reds could pack their bags and go off into the winter satisfied with a most successful season.

If there was a critical year in the history of The Big Red Machine, it was 1971. The 1970 champions stumbled badly, playing a mediocre 79–83 and finishing in a tie for fourth place.

Things began going wrong for the Reds in 1971 as early as January. While playing for the team's off-season basketball team in a game at Frankfort, Kentucky, Bobby Tolan suffered a ruptured Achilles tendon. The in-

Hal McRae (1968, 1970–1972), a talented outfielder whom the Cincinnati talent lode made expendable, had a long and productive career in the American League.

jury forced Tolan to miss the entire 1971 season (it also gave the front office second thoughts about the basketball team, which was soon disbanded.)

On May 29, 1971, the Reds engineered one of the most lopsided trades in their history. To the San Francisco Giants they sent minor-league pitcher Vern Geishert and little-used shortstop Frank Duffy in exchange for outfielder George Foster. The man who was to become the principal power dynamo of The Big Red Machine was then just twenty-two years old and had played just a handful of games for the Giants. Many Giant players were shocked when they learned of the trade.

"You didn't have to be a genius to see that George was going to be a hitter," one of the Giants said. "Why that trade was ever made, I'll never know." (The Foster debacle was part of a Giant pattern at the time: the club had already traded, or soon would, the three Alou brothers, Orlando Cepeda, and Gaylord Perry, receiving very little in return.)

The 1971 season saw Bench drop to a .238 average, 27 home runs, and 61 RBIs (a stunning drop of 87 from the year before). Concepcion hit a meager .205, and Carbo, .219. Rose batted .304, and May (39 home runs) and Perez (25) hit with power. The ace of the staff was the twenty-year-old Gullett (16–6), whom some Cincinnati fans were saying might be "our Koufax."

At the close of the season Howsam realized the team needed some restructuring. Where Crosley Field and its neighborly fences allowed the team to play a power game, Riverfront with its artificial surface and more distant targets called for some additional speed and defense. To this end, Howsam swung a most significant trade with Houston, on November 29, 1971. The Astros got slugger Lee May, second baseman Tommy Helms, and utility man Jimmy Stewart, in exchange for second baseman Joe Morgan, infielder Denis Menke, outfielders Ed Armbrister and Cesar Geronimo, and right-

Joe Morgan (1972–1979): "It turned out he was even better than we thought he was," said one Cincinnati scout.

hander Jack Billingham. With the arrival of Morgan, the Reds upgraded themselves from a good team to a great one.

Twenty-eight years old at the time of the trade, the 5-foot, 7-inch Morgan had been with Houston since 1963, playing a solid,

Gary Nolan.

hustling brand of ball. His highest average for the Astros was .285, in 1966. In 1971 he had batted .256. Nothing about his statistics was particularly eye catching, but the man's day-in, day-out style of play was.

"He was a hustler," one Cincinnati scout said of Morgan. "He played with intensity. He was an intelligent player. He had a good eye at the plate and drew a lot of walks, he had some power, he was quick and surehanded in the field, and he could steal bases. He was exactly what we needed, and then it turned out he was even better than we thought he was."

The new alignment had Perez taking over at first base, Morgan at second, Concepcion at short and Menke at third, Bench catching, and Geronimo, Rose, and a restored Tolan in the outfield. The top starters were Gullett, Nolan, Billingham, and young southpaw Ross Grimsley. Along with Carroll, Sparky's bullpen included two newcomers in Pedro Borbon and left-hander Tom Hall.

The Reds got off slowly in 1972, winning just 8 of their first 21 games. But then a 9-game May winning streak sent them off on a 65–30 tear that culminated in a fairly easy division title, 10½ games ahead of Houston and Los Angeles, who tied for second. Sparky's Machine, which had taken over first place for keeps on June 25, clinched the division on September 22.

For Johnny Bench it was a rip-roaring year of revival; on his way to his second MVP award, the Reds catcher led in home runs (40) and RBIs (125) and enjoyed the strength of his throwing arm in actuality and by reputation when only 25 bases were stolen against him in the 130 games he was behind the plate. (Johnny's "days off" were spent in left field and occasionally at third or first.)

Morgan was everything the Reds had hoped for, and more. He batted .292, led with 115 walks and 122 runs, hit 16 home runs, stole 58 bases, and committed just 8 errors as he led league second basemen with a .990 fielding average. Rose batted .307 and had the most hits (198). Perez, programmed to drive in runs, had 90 that year. The team's 140 stolen bases were the league's highest and its 110 errors the fewest.

Sparky's team won 95 games with only one pitcher notching as many as fifteen wins, Nolan, who was 15–5. Grimsley was 14–8 and Billingham 12–12. With the league's fewest complete games (25), it was evident that a strong bullpen was on the premises. Hall, obtained from the Minnesota Twins for Wayne Granger, was 10–1 with 7 saves; Borbon was 8–3 with 11 saves, and Carroll was 6–4 with 37 saves (at the time a new league record). Hampered by injuries, Gullett was 9–10.

Tom Hall (1972–1975), a slender left-handed reliever with a red-hot fastball, was 10–1 in 1972.

Left-hander Ross Grimsley (1971–1973), who was 14–8 in 1972.

The Eastern Division winners were the Pittsburgh Pirates, and the Reds fought them into the sunset in a full five-game series.

Pittsburgh beat Gullett in the opener, 5–1. Then the Reds, with Hall in relief, evened it with a 5–3 win, scoring four times in the top of the first.

With the contest now in Cincinnati, the Pirates went up by a game with a 3–2 win, beating Carroll. Then, in a do-or-die effort, Grimsley came through with a 2-hit, 7–1 victory, leaving the curtains parted for a decisive fifth game.

Sparky started Gullett and then followed with his bullpen trustworthies, Borbon, Hall,

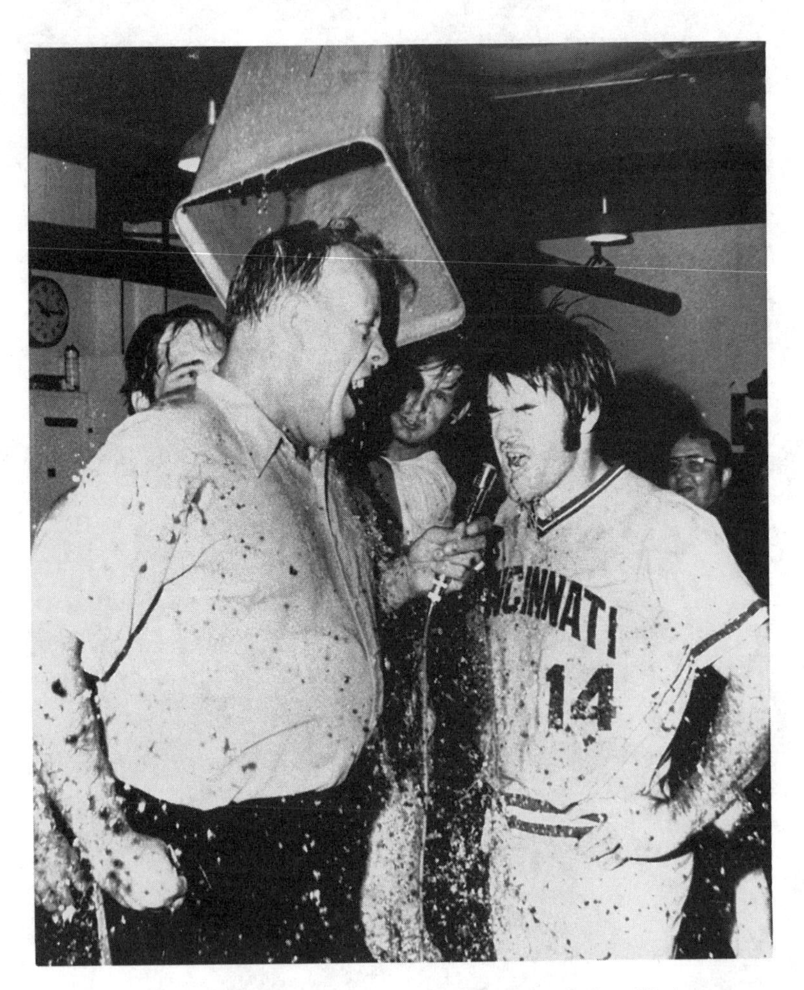

The Reds have just clinched the division title in 1972 and announcer Joe Nuxhall is interviewing Pete Rose as a can full of ice water is showered on them. The culprit is Darrel Chaney.

and Carroll. Going into the bottom of the ninth, the Reds found themselves perspiring under a 3–2 deficit, three outs away from a long, cold winter. Bench, however, quickly tied the game with a long, high home run to right field. Perez and Menke followed with singles, putting men on first and second. George Foster pinch-ran for Perez and promptly ran to third when Geronimo flied deep to right. With the winning run on third and one out, Darrel Chaney popped out. With Hal McRae batting for Carroll, Pirate reliever Bob Moose suddenly turned loose a wild pitch and Foster came racing home with the winning run, and the Reds had won their sixth pennant.

The 1972 World Series found the Reds matched with the Oakland Athletics, a team that featured outfielder Joe Rudi, shortstop Bert Campaneris, third baseman Sal Bando, and the club's greatest strength, a pitching staff of starters Catfish Hunter, Ken Holtzman, John ("Blue Moon") Odom, Vida Blue, and the great relief pitcher Rollie Fingers. (The team's big gun, Reggie Jackson, had suffered an injury in the pennant playoffs and did not play in the Series.)

This was the "One-Run World Series," with six of the seven games being decided by 1-run scores. It was also the Series when Oakland catcher–first baseman Gene Tenace, a .225 hitter with 5 home runs for the season, was alchemized for one week into the image of Babe Ruth.

The Series opened in Cincinnati with a 3–2 Oakland victory, Holtzman beating Nolan, with Tenace's 2 home runs driving in all the Oakland runs. Game 2 saw Hunter beat Grimsley, 2–1, with Rudi saving it for the A's with a sensational ninth-inning catch.

In Oakland now, Billingham gave the Reds their first victory when he outdueled Odom in a 1–0 pulse racer, the run scoring on Geronimo's seventh-inning single. The A's then took a formidable three games to one lead by winning Game 4, 3–2, scoring 2 in the bottom of the ninth on 3 pinch-hit singles, making A's skipper Dick Williams look like a genius. Game 5 continued the 1-run-margin pattern as the Reds stayed alive when Grimsley beat Fingers, 5–4, on Rose's ninth-inning single.

Back in Cincinnati, the Reds tied the Series with an 8–1 win, Grimsley beating Blue (Grimsley pitched just $1\frac{2}{3}$ innings in picking up his two wins). The A's won the finale, 3–2, with Hunter gaining the decision over Borbon, both in relief. (Not a single complete game was pitched in the Series.)

In a light-hitting Series—both teams had identical 46-for-220 records and .209 batting averages—the difference was Tenace. He tied

(Above) Lee May thundering home to score in Game 2 of the 1970 World Series. The catcher is Baltimore's Elrod Hendricks.

(Above right) Victory and elation: Clay Carroll has just registered the final out in Cincinnati's victory over Baltimore in Game 4 of the 1970 World Series.

(Below right) Johnny Bench *(left)* and Clay Carroll after beating the Orioles in Game 4 of the 1970 Series. Carroll (1968–1975) was one of the best of all Cincinnati relief pitchers.

(Below) Oakland's Gene Tenace, who tormented the Reds throughout the 1972 World Series, is shown here hitting the first of the 4 home runs he struck in the Series. It came against Gary Nolan in the second inning of Game 1.

Dan Driessen (1973–1984) batted .301 in his rookie year.

a Series record with 4 home runs, batted .348, and drove in 9 of the 16 Oakland runs. For the Reds, Perez had 10 hits (most in the Series) and batted .435.

The Reds repeated as Western Division champions in 1973, but the caprices of divisional play came to bear and they lost to an East-winning New York Mets team that had barely won its division with an 82–79 record. The Reds outhit the Mets in every offensive department, made fewer errors, and in stolen bases had 148 to New York's 27. What the Mets did have were three excellent starters in Tom Seaver and left-handers Jerry Koosman and Jon Matlack and a strong closer in lefty Tug McGraw.

Cincinnati's division title had been won with a tremendous second-half surge. Trailing the Dodgers by 11 games on July 1, Sparky's boys took off and won 60 of their last 86, ending with 99 victories and a 3 1/2-game lead at the end.

The June 15 acquisition of left-hander Fred Norman from San Diego had proved most beneficial, the new man going 12–6 for the Reds, helping fill the void created by the loss of Gary Nolan, who would be idled for the next two years with a bad arm. Billingham was 19–10, with 7 shutouts, and Gullett, 18–8. Borbon, Hall, and Carroll again were a strong relief corps.

Rose had a superb year, one that earned him a MVP plaque, taking his third batting title with a .338 mark and leading the league with a hefty 230 hits. Perez had 27 homers; Morgan, 26; and Bench, 25. The Reds added another good bat when they brought up first baseman–third baseman Dan Driessen, who batted .301. Another new man, Ken Griffey, broke into 25 games and batted .384.

The playoff series with the Mets opened at Riverfront and the Reds took the opener in dazzling style. With Tom Seaver outdueling Billingham 1–0 in the bottom of the eighth, Rose, who had hit only 5 home runs all year, whacked one to tie the score. Then in the bottom of the ninth, Bench hit one out to give the Reds a 2–1 win. Matlack tied the series at a game apiece, beating Gullett, 5–0, in Game 2.

In Game 3, at Shea Stadium, the Mets tore into Grimsley and four relievers for a 9–2 victory behind Koosman. The most memorable feature of this game was a fifth-inning brawl between Rose and Mets shortstop Bud Harrelson, provoked by what Harrelson felt was an overly enthusiastic slide by Pete into second base. When he went out to left field after the inning, Pete became the target for whatever wasn't nailed down in that part of the park, and it took Sparky's removal of his team from the field before the fans calmed down.

In the face of cascades of boos and cat-

(RIGHT) Jack Billingham (1972–1977), twice a 19-game winner for Sparky.

(LEFT) Billy Plummer (1970–1977), Cincinnati's backup catcher during Johnny Bench's heyday years.

The Pete Rose–Bud Harrelson brawl at Shea Stadium during the 1973 pennant playoffs between the Reds and New York Mets.

Pete Rose, one by one, until there were 4,256 of them.

calls, Pete Rose showed his mettle the next day when he hit a twelfth-inning home run that gave the Reds and Carroll a 2–1 victory, tying the series. But in the finale, Seaver and the Mets rolled to an easy 7–2 pennant clincher over Billingham.

The Reds won 98 games in 1974, but that was a year when the Los Angeles Dodgers were not to be denied; Walter Alston's men won 102 and finished 4 ahead of a Cincinnati club that could never quite catch up. Behind by as many as 10½ games as late as July 10, the Reds pulled to within 1½ of the first-place Dodgers but just couldn't make it all the way back.

Bench hit 33 home runs that year and with 129 RBIs led the league for the third time. Perez hit 28 long ones and drove in 101 runs, and Morgan hit 22 homers and stole 58 bases. (The most notable home run struck at Riverfront in 1974 was the one hit by Hank Aaron on opening day, April 4; it was the 714th of his career, tying him with Babe Ruth on the career list.) Billingham was the staff's most prolific winner with a 19–11 record, Gullett was 17–11, and to an already deep and talented bullpen were added two more youngsters, left-hander Will McEnaney and Rawley Eastwick. They were joining a club that was getting ready to begin a virtually irresistible two-year flight through the universe of baseball.

F·I·F·T·E·E·N

THE MACHINE IN OVERDRIVE

ON the morning of May 21, 1975, the Cincinnati Reds had a 20–20 record and, despite an obvious abundance of talent, were like a team floating amiably to nowhere. Then, suddenly, as if undergoing a total personality change, the club went on to win 41 of their next 50, and by the end of the season their summer's work was 108–54, meaning that from that 20–20 moment in May they had played 88–34 baseball.

Sparky's rip-roaring machine took over first place on June 7 and were never dislodged, playing 21–7 ball in June; 20–9, in July; and 21–8, in August. Among the club's many high-caliber achievements this season were:

A National League record 64 games won at home

A major-league record 15 consecutive errorless games

A major-league record for fewest unearned runs charged to a pitching staff: 40

An .823 percentage rate of successful stolen bases (168 steals)

Some of the main gears of The Big Red Machine *(left to right):* Tony Perez, Johnny Bench, Joe Morgan, Pete Rose.

Joe Morgan, rising to an MVP year, batted .327 and drew more walks than any player in Cincinnati history, 132. Bench hit 28 home runs and drove in 110 runs, Perez had 20 homers and 109 RBIs. Rose batted .317 and delivered 210 hits; Griffey, .305; and Foster, .300 with 23 home runs.

It was because of the laudable team spirit shown by Rose that Foster was finally able to get into the lineup. Rose had been content in the outfield (winning all three of his batting titles while playing there), but the club wanted a position for Foster, who could only play the outfield, and third base was the only spot on the team not already filled by a star-

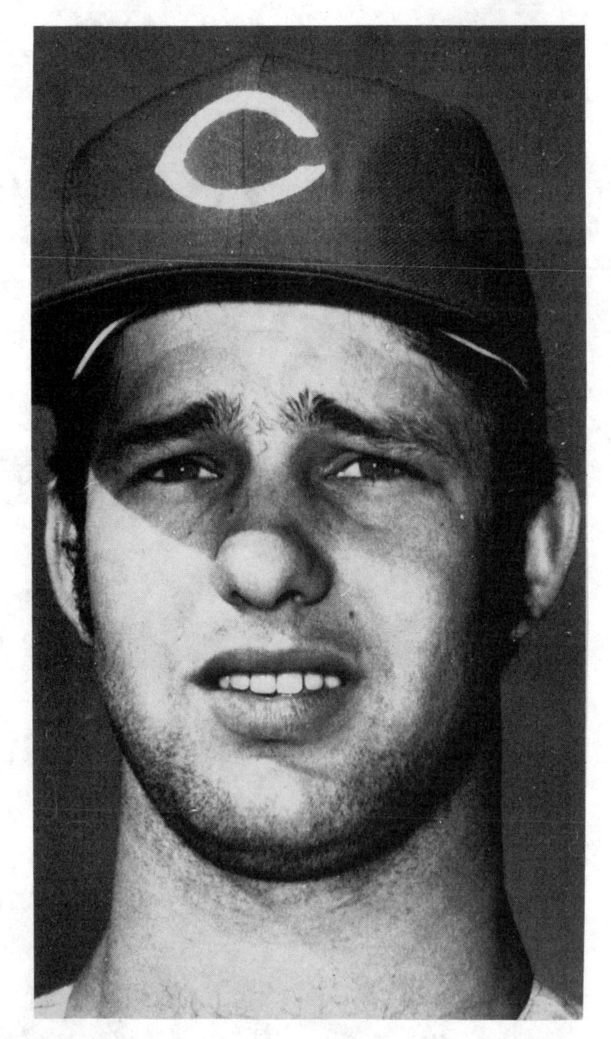

Left-hander Don Gullett (1970–1976). The hard-throwing, injury-prone pitcher was 18–8 in 1973.

ring regular. So without complaint, Rose moved to third base, where he would play for the next four years.

Again Sparky won a ton of games without a pitcher winning more than fifteen. Gullet surely would have been a bigger winner, but the ace lefty, always injury prone, lost the better part of two months with a fracture of the thumb on his pitching hand, and ended the season at 15–4. Nolan, making a strong comeback from two years of injury-forced inactivity, was 15–9, and Billingham was 15–10. Fred Norman, Clay Kirby, and Pat Darcy each won in double figures, while the deep bullpen of Borbon, Eastwick, McEnaney, and Carroll saved 50 games. The staff had only 22 complete games, at one point in the season going 45 straight games without a starter going all the way.

Reflecting a club that made just 102 errors all season, the Reds had four Gold Glove winners: Bench, Morgan, Concepcion, and center fielder Cesar Geronimo.

The Reds clinched the division on September 7, with their final margin an emphatic 20 games ahead of the second-place Dodgers.

The pennant playoff series against the Eastern Division–winning Pirates was simply another forum for Cincinnati dominance, the Reds burning out the Pirates in three straight by scores of 8–3, 6–1, and, in ten innings, 5–3. The final game saw a powerful performance by Pittsburgh's rookie left-hander John Candelaria, who fanned 14 in 7⅔ innings.

Southpaw Fred Norman (1973–1979), a steady winner for The Big Red Machine.

Will McEnaney (1974–1976), one of the relief aces of the 1975–1976 pennant winners.

Reliever Rawley Eastwick (1974–1977), who led the league in saves in 1975 and 1976.

Right-hander Pedro Borbon (1970–1979), a long-time mainstay of the Cincinnati bullpen.

Cesar Geronimo (1972–1980), Cincinnati's brilliant defensive center fielder, batted .307 in 1976.

Ken Griffey (1973–1981, 1988–1990), a steady .300 stick in the Reds outfield, with a high of .336 in 1976.

George Foster (1971–1981) led in RBIs three straight years.

The Reds then plunged into what many have described as the greatest World Series of all time. The Boston Red Sox had won their division and then upset the three-time world champion Oakland Athletics in three straight playoff games. This exceptionally strong Sox team included catcher Carlton Fisk; shortstop Rick Burleson; first baseman Cecil Cooper; third baseman Rico Petrocelli; and outfielders Fred Lynn, Carl Yastrzemski, Dwight Ewans, and Jim Rice (who sat out the Series with an injury). Boston's front-line pitching including Rick Wise, Luis Tiant, and left-hander Bill Lee.

The Series opened at Boston's venerable Fenway Park with Tiant giving the Sox a leg up with a 6–0 blanking, beating Gullett, with all the scoring being done in the bottom of the seventh. The Reds tied it the next day, 3–2, thanks to a 2-run top of the ninth, put together on clutch hits by Bench, Concepcion, and Griffey, with Eastwick winning.

Back home at Riverfront, the Reds won Game 3 in ten innings, 6–5, after dissipating a 5–2 lead, Eastwick again winning in relief. In Game 4, the Reds lost for a second time to Tiant, who went all the way in a gritty 5–4 victory, throwing 163 pitches. Game 5 saw the emergence of Tony Perez as a Series factor. After going 0 for 15, the team's most consistent RBI man broke out with 2 home runs and 4 RBIs, helping Gullett to a 6–2 victory. Up 3 games to 2, the Reds returned to Boston, looking to wrap up the team's first world championship since Bill McKechnie's boys of 1940.

Game 6 of the 1975 World Series was one for baseball's balladeers. The Sox took a 3–0 lead in the bottom of the first. The Reds tied it with 3 in the top of the fifth, then went ahead with 2 in the seventh and another in the eighth. Then in the bottom of the eighth, Bernie Carbo, whom the Reds had brought to the big leagues and was now with Boston, pinch-hit a stunning 3-run homer that tied it. In the bottom of the ninth, Boston loaded the bases with none out, only to have Foster take a fly ball and throw the runner out at home. In the top of the eleventh, a sizzling leaping catch by right fielder Dwight Evans deprived Morgan of a probable 2-run homer. Finally, in the bottom of the twelfth, Carlton Fisk pasted Pat Darcy's first pitch against the left

That's Johnny Bench dialing long distance against the Red Sox in the fourth inning of Game 3 of the 1975 World Series. The homer was a two-run shot. The catcher is Carlton Fisk, the umpire Larry Barnett.

Carlton Fisk in semaphore communication with the home-run ball that ended the famous Game 6 of the 1975 World Series. Pitcher Pat Darcy and Johnny Bench can only watch and wait.

Red Sox pitcher Bill Lee gazes pensively as Tony Perez circles the bases behind him. Tony's home-run shot came in the sixth inning of the seventh game of the 1975 Series. The blow put the Reds back in the game.

Joe Morgan hitting the looping single that drove in the game-winning run in the top of the ninth inning of the final game of the 1975 Series.
The pitcher is Jim Burton, the catcher Carlton Fisk, the umpire Art Frantz.

Cincinnati's Fountain Square is packed with fans cheering the Reds players and celebrating the city's first world championship in 35 years.

field foul pole, giving Boston an emotion-drenched 7–6 victory and leaving the stage lit for a seventh game.

Game 7 saw Boston again jump out to a 3–0 lead, but by the top of the seventh it was tied 3–3, thanks in part to a 2-run Perez homer. In the top of the ninth, the Reds scored the final run of the 1975 baseball season when Morgan dropped a soft 2-out single into center field, scoring Griffey. With McEnaney on the mound, the Reds retired the Red Sox in the bottom of the ninth and The Machine had gone all the way.

High on the list of Cincinnati's Series heroes were two men who performed in their accustomed style: Rose had the most hits (10) and Perez, despite his slow start, the most runs batted in (7).

The Reds were a near unanimous choice to repeat in 1976 and this mighty team—perhaps the greatest in National League history—would not disappoint. The 1976 model of The Big Red Machine won fewer games than its predecessor (102) but was its superior in every other respect. This bruising outfit led the National League in home runs, triples, doubles, runs, runs batted in, batting average, slugging, stolen bases, and bases on balls; made the fewest errors; and had the highest fielding percentage. The team's .280 batting average was their best in 46 years and their 857 runs and 1,599 hits established all-time club records. Another record also went into the books—the club's ledgers this time—when 2,629,708 satisfied customers gave the franchise a new attendance peak.

Individual league leaders included Rose in runs (130), hits (215), and doubles (42); Foster in RBIs (121); and Morgan in slugging (.576). Griffey, a .336 hitter, lost the batting crown on the season's final day to Chicago's Bill Madlock. Morgan, for the second year in

Pete Rose scoring the Pete Rose way.

a row, was MVP. Griffey, Morgan, Rose, Foster, and Geronimo were .300 hitters, helping to pick up for Bench's subpar .234 season.

Again Sparky didn't have a pitcher with more than fifteen wins, but he did have seven chuckers win in double figures, unprecedented in the National League. Led by Nolan's 15, they were Pat Zachry, Billingham, Norman, Gullett, young right-hander Santo Alcala, and Eastwick. Zachry, a tall, thin right-hander, tied that year for Rookie of the Year honors with San Diego reliever Butch Metzger.

After beating the Dodgers at Riverfront on May 30, the Reds moved into first place and took out a lease for the rest of the season. Their final margin of victory was 10 games ahead of the Dodgers.

Perhaps no game more typified the strength and self-confidence of The Big Red Machine than the one played between the Reds and Cubs at Wrigley Field on August 11, 1976. Trailing 10–1 after three innings, Sparky's men came back to take a 13–10 victory in ten innings.

Nothing was going to stand in the way of the 1976 Reds, and nothing did. In postseason play there wasn't a single misstep. In the pennant playoffs, this time against the Phillies, the Reds made it a one-way street, winning three straight, albeit not without a bit of dramatics.

After Gullett won the first game, 6–3, and Zachry the second, 6–2, the Phillies forced the Reds to break a sweat. Played at Riverfront, the game had the Phillies up by 3–0 in the bottom of the seventh. The Reds then scored four times to take the lead, but the Phillies fought back and going into the bottom of the ninth led by 6–4. Then Foster led off with a homer, followed by a game-tier from Bench, who had a flair for dramatic home runs. Concepcion walked and eventually came around to score on a hit by Griffey and the Reds had another pennant.

Joe Morgan, Cincinnati's two-time MVP.

Pat Zachry (1976–1977), cowinner of Rookie of the Year honors in 1976.

The World Series was strictly a Machine-tooled affair. Billy Martin's Yankees were never in it. The Reds took the first two games at Riverfront, 5–1 and 4–3, Gullett and Billingham winning. Going on to Yankee Stadium, the Reds dispatched the New Yorkers with minimum effort, 6–2 for Zachry and 7–2 with Nolan. The finale was dominated by Bench, who hit 2 home runs and drove in 5 runs.

The October cakewalk made Sparky's Reds the first National League team to win successive world championships since the 1921 and 1922 New York Giants. In the opinion of many baseball people, there had never been a National League aggregation the equal of the 1975–1976 Cincinnati Reds, with the possible exception of the Brooklyn Dodger teams of the 1950s. In any event, on anyone's list of baseball's all-time elite teams, these Cincinnati Reds would without a doubt have representation.

The first crack in The Big Red Machine came on November 18, 1976, when Don Gullett, taking advantage of the free-agent era, now just dawning, signed with the Yankees (with whom his injury-haunted career would come to an abrupt end after little more than a year).

Another vital gear was stripped from The Machine a month later when Howsam made an unfortunate trade. The deal saw Perez and McEnaney go to the Montreal Expos for pitchers Woody Fryman and Dale Murray. It wasn't just that neither Fryman nor Murray

Johnny Bench.

Tony Perez, RBIs were his specialty.

brought much sunshine to Cincinnati, but that in trading Perez the Reds were dispatching someone who was more than a good ball player. Tony was, by all accounts, a most positive presence in the clubhouse, popular with and respected by everyone.

Howsam's rationale for the trade (which he later admitted was "my biggest mistake") was that a spot had to be opened up for Dan Driessen, whose best position was first base. Driessen was nine years younger than the thirty-four-year-old Perez, and while Dan was to give the Reds some decent years, the team would sorely miss Perez (who was going to go on hitting for the next four or five years, methodically driving in runs for Montreal and then the Boston Red Sox and the Philadelphia Phillies before returning to Cincinnati to finish out his playing career).

After taking five division titles in seven years, the Reds slipped to second place in 1977, 10 games behind Tom Lasorda's Dodgers. This was despite a herculean year by Foster, who belted a soaring 52 home runs and drove in 149 runs, each a league-leading

George Foster, 52 big ones in 1977.

figure and each a new club record. The Reds left fielder also led in slugging (.631) and runs (124) and that fall became the sixth Cincinnati player in eight years to win the MVP Award. George received some strong support from Bench (31 homers, 109 RBIs), Griffey (.318), Driessen (.300), and Rose (.311). Pete's 204 hits put him over the 200 mark for the ninth time, tying Ty Cobb's major-league record (which Pete would break two years later while playing for the Phillies).

A spectacular June 15 trade with the New York Mets brought the Reds the league's premier right-hander. Tom Seaver had been engaged with the Mets front office in an acrimonious dispute over contract renegotiation, which culminated in the trade of their three-time Cy Young award winner. In exchange for the ace, the Reds sent New York pitcher Pat Zachry, second baseman Doug Flynn, and outfielders Steve Henderson and Dan Norman.

Joe Morgan.

Tom Seaver (1977–1982).

On the same day, the Reds traded Gary Nolan to California and Rawley Eastwick to St. Louis, getting little in return. (Nolan was about through and Eastwick was never again as effective as he had been for Cincinnati.)

Seaver anchored the Reds staff like the champion he was, from June 15 on logging a 14–3 record.

The 1977 Reds displayed baseball's most efficient glovework, setting a major-league fielding record with a .984 team average, committing a record-low 95 errors, and setting still another league mark with 94 errorless games. Joe Morgan established a new standard for second basemen with just 5

Pete Rose, all set for another whack.

errors (since tied). From July 6, 1977, through April 22, 1978, Joe played 91 games and handled 410 chances without a bobble. (The 91 games were a record, broken by Ryne Sandberg in 1990.)

In 1978, the Reds again finished second. A strong 19–8 September charge had been unable to make up the ground lost by a 10–18 August, and the shortfall was 2 1/2 games. Injuries suffered by Morgan and Bench curtailed the effectiveness of these stars, but Foster turned out another big season, again leading in home runs (40) and RBIs (120), giving him three successive RBI crowns, tying an impressive major-league record, coheld with heavyweights like Cobb and Ruth in the American League and Wagner, Hornsby, and Medwick in the National. Concepcion's .301 average made him the first Reds shortstop since Joe Tinker in 1913 to bat .300. At 16–14, Seaver topped the staff.

The most widely heard noises of Cincinnati's 1978 season came from the tireless bat of Pete Rose. The Reds thirty-seven-year-old, nonstop hustler joined an elite group on May 5, 1978, when he rapped out his 3,000th career hit, a fifth-inning single off Montreal's Steve Rogers. A 3,000th hit becomes an inevitability, with anticipation dominating suspense; what Pete began on June 14, 1978 was something else. His two hits in that day's game against the Cubs launched a hitting streak that would rivet the attention of baseball fans throughout the middle of the summer. On July 18, Pete made it 31 in a row, breaking an ancient club record set in 1898 by one Elmer Smith. On July 25, he hit in his 38th straight game, breaking the National League record set by the Braves' Tommy Holmes in 1945.

As Pete went on, rapping his line drives, visions of Joe DiMaggio's 1941 56-game streak began looming on the horizon. But that mythic record was not to be broken. On August 1, after a genuinely thrilling 44-game run, Rose was stopped (0 for 4) in Atlanta by pitchers Larry McWilliams and Gene Garber. The streak, second longest in baseball history, was a blazing symbol of the career-long consistency of Pete Rose, who would ultimately become baseball's most prolific collector of base hits.

Earlier, on June 16, Seaver had pitched what would be the only no-hitter of his Hall-of-Fame career, stopping the Cardinals by a 4–0 score.

The postseason brought Cincinnati a pair of jarring departures. In April, Bob Howsam had eased into semiretirement as vice-chairman of the club's board of directors, with his long-time assistant Dick Wagner taking over as president and chief executive officer. On November 28, 1978, Wagner flew to California to see Sparky Anderson. The skipper was expecting a "State of the Team" meeting. But it was something else. Wagner told Sparky a change was being made, that the Reds were to have a new manager. After a remarkably successful nine-year tenure, during which his teams had won five division titles, four pennants, two world championships, and had three second-place finishes, Sparky was gone (soon to resurface as manager of the Detroit Tigers). His successor was John McNamara, previously skipper at Oakland and San Diego.

On December 5, 1978, Cincinnati baseball lost another of its icons. After being unable to come to terms with the Reds, Pete Rose became a free agent and signed a four-year, $3.2 million contract with the Philadelphia Phillies.

Right-hander Doug Bair (1978–1981), gave the Reds some strong relief work.

John McNamara, who managed the Reds from 1979 to 1982.

Although it had lost some of its biggest wheels, The Big Red Machine still had enough high-octane fuel in the tank to take a division title in 1979, as McNamara's club edged out Houston by 1½ games to win the West for the sixth time in the 1970s.

Seaver (16–6) and right-hander Mike LaCoss (14–8) led a starting contingent that was ably abetted by relievers Doug Bair and Tom Hume. Injuries held Foster to 121 games and probably cost him a shot at a record-breaking fourth straight RBI crown (he had 98 to 116 for the leader, San Diego's Dave

Ray Knight, who was given the unenviable task of replacing Pete Rose at third base, played for the Reds in 1974 and from 1977 to 1981, with .318 in 1979 his best year.

Winfield). The team's top hitter was Rose's replacement at third base, Ray Knight (.318).

The Reds' 90 victories were fewer than any of Sparky's winners had compiled, but they proved enough to win the West, thanks primarily to a blistering 19–7 August, during which Seaver completed an 11-game winning streak. The Reds took over first place for keeps on September 11 and clinched the division on September 28, two days before the end of the season.

Twice before, in 1970 and 1975, the Reds had met the Eastern Division champion Pittsburgh Pirates in the pennant playoffs and each time paved the Pirates under in three. The two clubs met again in 1979 and there was another sweep, but this time the strong hand belonged to Pittsburgh.

In the opener, the Pirates won in eleven innings, 5–2, on Willie Stargell's 3-run homer, Hume losing in relief of Seaver, who had worked a strong eight innings. The second game was another edge-of-the-blade loss for the Reds, 3–2 in ten innings. The third and last game was all Pittsburgh, 7–1.

Although ending on this note of disappointment, for Cincinnati baseball the 1979 season had brought its half-measure of victory; and for those inclined to make a summation of the full decade, there were a plethora of bright moments to recall, great stars to celebrate, and ever-sweet victories to savor, for the Reds had riddled the record book and enjoyed one of the most successful decades of any team in baseball history.

S·I·X·T·E·E·N

INTO THE 1980S

THE Reds began the new decade by making a run at another division title, but fell short, finishing in third place, 3 1/2 games behind Houston. The Reds began the season with 8 straight victories and had a 13–6 April, but then two sub-.500 months removed some of the gloss.

Considering the many injuries the team suffered during the season, John McNamara did a good job in keeping his club in contention. Right-hander Bill Bonham, penciled in as a regular starter, was KO'd for most of the year with a shoulder injury. Seaver went on the disabled list for the first time in his career, missing most of the month of July with shoulder problems, ending with a 10–8 record. Right-hander Frank Pastore, the club's big winner with a 13–7 record, missed almost two full months with an injury. The time lost by these pitchers did have one positive consequence—it opened up the gates of opportunity for young right-handed fastballer Mario Soto, who posted a 10–8 mark, with nine of his wins coming after the All-Star break.

A vital spark was lost to the team when Joe Morgan declared free agency and signed with Houston, helping that club to the division title. Junior Kennedy and Ron Oester filled in adequately at second, but Morgan's leadership was missed.

Outfielder Dave Collins turned in an outstanding season, batting .303 and stealing 79 bases, two under the old club high set by Bob Bescher in 1911.

Johnny Bench tied Bill Dickey's major-league record by catching more than 100

Frank Pastore (1979–1985); his top year was 13–7 in 1980.

Light-footed outfielder Dave Collins (1978–1981, 1987–1989) stole 79 bases in 1980.

games for the thirteenth straight year. But this long, grueling service at baseball's most demanding position had taken its toll. The accumulated aches and pains and bangs and bruises of more than 1,700 games behind the plate led Bench to announce that this would be his last year as a catcher, leading Reds fans to wonder where their thirty-three-year-old future Hall of Famer would be posted the following year. On July 15, 1980, Bench had broken Yogi Berra's home-run record for catchers by belting number 314 (Johnny had hit 33 others while playing other positions).

In 1981, McNamara's team played to the best won–lost record in the division, but spent the postseason watching the action on television. This was because of the players' strike that shut down the baseball season from June 12 through August 9. When play resumed, the owners came up with the bizarre notion of declaring a split season, with the winners of the two halves meeting in division playoffs preceding the regular pennant playoffs.

Having just made the force on Chicago's Jerry Martin and thrown on to first for the double play, Dave Concepcion is now doing the prudent thing.

At the time of the strike, the Reds had a 35–21 record and were $^{1}/_{2}$ game behind the Dodgers. When play resumed, the Reds posted a second-half mark of 31–21, finishing $1^{1}/_{2}$ games behind the Astros. Cincinnati's overall 66–42 mark was superior to anyone else's in the division, but under the harebrained split-season format it earned them nothing.

Tom Seaver had an excellent 14–2 season, Soto was 12–9, and Tom Hume was the bullpen bulwark. A broken ankle limited Johnny Bench to 52 games and when he did play it was primarily at first base. Griffey, Concepcion, and catcher Joe Nolan were .300 hitters, and despite missing one-third of the schedule, Foster drove in 90 runs, one fewer than league leader Mike Schmidt.

Tom Seaver.

Right-hander Tom Hume, who anchored the Reds bullpen from 1977 to 1985. He pitched briefly for the Reds in 1987.

After the season, the Reds underwent a series of roster changes that stripped some more gears from the old Machine and seriously depleted what had been a strong offensive lineup.

Fearing that they were about to lose Griffey to free agency, the Reds on November 4, 1981 traded him to the Yankees for two minor-league pitchers. Then, having to find a place in the lineup for Bench, the Reds on December 18 traded Ray Knight to Houston for Cesar Cedeno. On December 21, Dave Collins became a free agent and signed with the Yankees. Finally, on February 10, 1982, unwilling to meet Foster's salary request, the Reds traded him to the Mets for a trio of players who contributed little to the Cincinnati cause.

Cesar Cedeno, the veteran outfielder was with the Reds from 1982 to 1985.

So it should have come as no surprise when in 1982 the Reds took a sudden and precipitous dive through the standings, losing a franchise-high 101 games and crumbling in last place. With illness and injuries hobbling him, Seaver was a wretched 5–13; Mario Soto filled the ace's role with a 14–13 record and a new club high of 274 strikeouts.

The first victim of the team's descent was, inevitably (and probably unfairly), John McNamara, who was fired on July 21 and replaced by his third-base coach Russ Nixon, who had caught in the American League from 1957 to 1968. Unfortunately for Nixon, he had taken on a team that was in the midst of a period of decline, a condition that at one time or another will numb the efforts of every ball club.

In December, Seaver was traded back to the Mets for right-hander Charlie Puleo and two minor leaguers.

It wasn't far into the 1983 season before Cincinnati fans realized that the new season was going to bear a striking resemblance to the previous year's. While the club lost fewer games in 1983 (88), it hardly mattered in the final standings, which once more found the Reds bottomed out in last place.

The team had one genuine high achiever in Soto, who was 17–13, with 242 strikeouts and 2.70 ERA. With a 10–6 record, lefty Joe

Right-hander Bruce Berenyi (1980–1984), whose 18 losses in 1982 were most in the league.

Price was the only other pitcher to win in double figures.

For the thirty-five-year-old Johnny Bench, who divided his playing time between first and third bases, it was his farewell season, so announced in July. This turned the Reds into a sort of caravan in the latter part of the season, visiting each port of call and hearing yet again the local fans' final tributes and cheers of appreciation for the man who had been perhaps the greatest of all catchers. Bench's retirement left Dave Concepcion and Dan Driessen as the last members of the awesome 1976 championship team still with the Reds.

The biggest changes for the 1984 Cincinnati Reds came in the front office and in the manager's office. The new owner was Marge Schott, a local automobile dealer, who bought out the interests of the Williams brothers, James and William. In Schott—"Marge" to everyone—the club was getting an owner who through her informality and colorful personality was soon to become one of the game's most well-known executives. Just before divesting themselves of the club, the Williams brothers had fired Dick Wagner, whose moves (beginning with the dismissal of Sparky Anderson) had done little to strengthen the Reds. Bob Howsam was induced out of semiretirement to replace Wagner, and when Schott took over the club, Howsam remained in place.

Mario Soto (1977–1988) was 18–7 in 1984.

Southpaw Joe Price (1980–1986), who alternated between starting and relieving for the Reds.

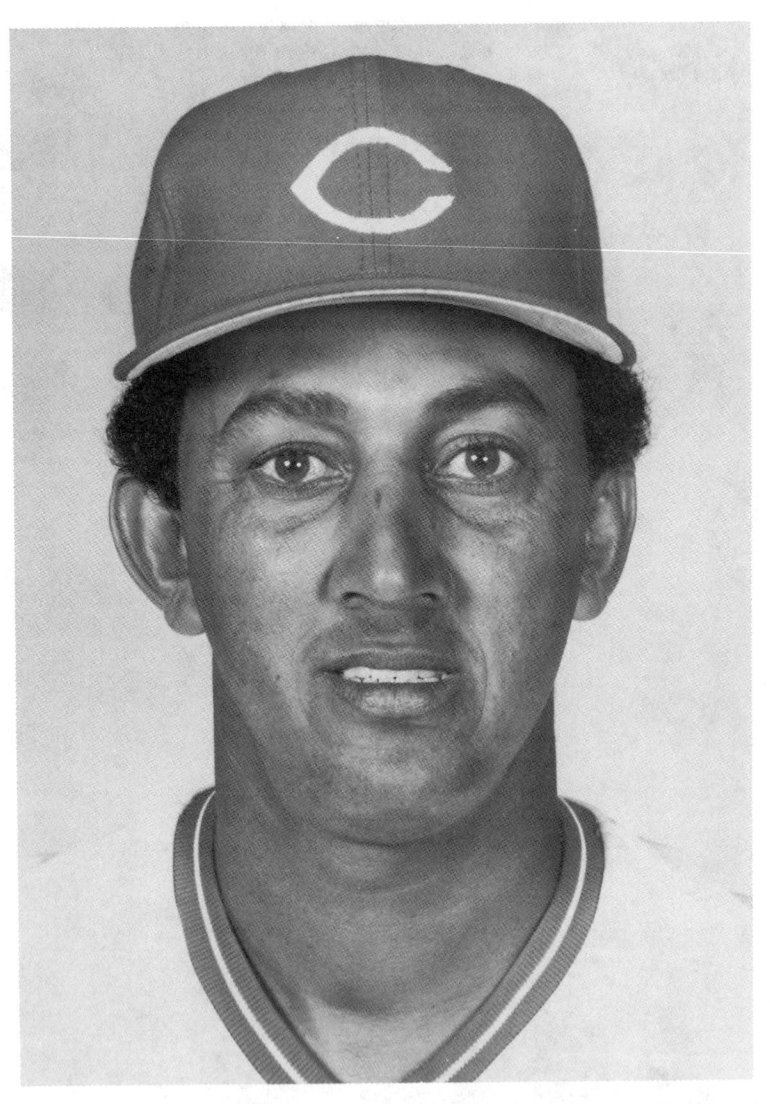

Dave Concepcion: 19 years in a Cincinnati uniform.

Marge Schott soon proved herself a rarity among big-league club owners: she was a sentimentalist, and she proved it not with vaporous declarations but by action. Russ Nixon had been dismissed after the 1983 season and replaced by Vern Rapp, one-time skipper of the Cardinals. But Marge wanted some of the old-time glory back, and wanted it back right now.

After playing five years with the Phillies, Pete Rose had signed with Montreal, with whom he was engaging in his avowed pursuit—the all-time hit record of 4,191, held by Ty Cobb. Now forty-three years old, Pete was finding the bat a bit heavier to swing, the pitching a little better than it would have seemed a decade before, and his reflexes not as responsive. Nevertheless, Pete had the record in the cross hairs and there was no way he was going to leave baseball before breaking it.

Believing that Pete should never have been allowed to leave Cincinnati in the first place, Schott told Howsam to get him back. Montreal agreed to let Pete go (it was as though they recognized that they possessed some venerable treasure that rightfully belonged to the city of Cincinnati). So on August 16, 1984, the deal was made (utility infielder Tom Lawless went to the Expos) and Pete Rose's circle home had been completed: from Cincinnati to Philadelphia to Montreal and

Outfielder Gary Redus (1982–1985) stole 48 bases in 1984 and again the next year.

Pete Rose took over as Reds manager late in the 1984 season and left amid the troubles of 1989.

Pete Rose collecting base hit number 4,192, breaking Ty Cobb's all-time record.

back to Cincinnati. Vern Rapp was dismissed and Pete became what had once been common in baseball but now was something of an anomaly—the playing manager (although hardly playing on a regular basis anymore). At the close of the season, Pete had 4,097 hits, 95 short of breaking Cobb's record.

The Reds finished fifth in 1984, with little to show for the season beyond Soto's 18–7 record and 94 RBIs from free-agent signer Dave Parker, Pittsburgh's former two-time batting champion.

When the 1985 baseball season began, there were office pools all around the country centered on the date when Pete Rose would get what the tough old veteran himself called "the big knock"—hit number 4,192, the one that would topple the ghost of Ty Cobb from its fifty-seven-year-old pedestal. If you had September 11 in the pool, you were a winner, for it was on that date that Pete Rose, in the twenty-third year of a career that had made him a folk hero, delivered the hit that changed what had long been considered one of the

Outfielder Eddie Milner (1980–1986) swiped 41 bases in 1983.

record book's most unassailable entries. The famous hit came at Riverfront against San Diego's Eric Show, when in the bottom of the first inning Pete slashed a 2–1 pitch into left-center for a single. Baseball researchers, an indefatigable and imaginative band of romantics, who leave no base unlifted in their search for analogies, anniversaries, coincidences, and ironies, discovered that it was fifty-seven years to the day that Cobb played his last major-league game.

Along with all the Roman candles attendant on Rose's record quest was a surprisingly strong second-place finish for the club, $5\frac{1}{2}$ games behind the Dodgers. With Soto dropping to 12–15, the team found a pleasant surprise in rookie left-hander Tom Browning, whose 20–9 record made him the first freshman to win 20 since Bob Grim of the Yankees in 1954. Hard-nosed southpaw John Franco was 12–3 out of the pen, with 12 saves, and right-hander Ted Power notched 27 saves.

Dave Parker turned in what many thought should have been an MVP season (he ran second in the voting to Willie McGee), batting .312 and leading in RBIs with 125. Forty-three-year-old Tony Perez, back with the club for a last hurrah, warmed up some of the old nostalgia with a .328 average in 72 games.

The 1985 season began what for the Reds was to become a second-place rut: the club was going to finish in the bridesmaid position

Ron Oester (1978–), who did well as Joe Morgan's replacement at second base.

Tom Browning (1984–), Cincinnati's rookie 20-game winner in 1985.

through 1988. A 6–19 start in 1986 put the team at a season-long disadvantage and it took some sharp playing to enable them to post an 86–76 record at the end, leaving them 10 games behind Houston.

The club's top hitter in 1986 was veteran third baseman Buddy Bell (.278), acquired the previous summer from the Texas Rangers. Parker, although dropping to .273, drove in 116 runs, while the team introduced a scintillating new talent in center fielder Eric Davis, a "full service" player who could do it all. Burdened with the label of "the next Willie Mays," the twenty-four-year-old Davis batted .277, hit 27 home runs (some for enormous distances), and stole 80 bases (one under the team record) in 132 games. Along with Davis, the Reds began introducing into the lineup shortstop Barry Larkin and outfielder Kal Daniels, both twenty-two years old and brimming with talent (Daniels batted .320 in 74 games).

Bill Bergesch, a former Yankee front-office executive, was now the Reds' general man-

Dave Parker (1984–1987), the RBI leader in 1985.

Dave Parker, contact seems imminent.

ager, and he had swung a good off-season deal, getting right-hander Bill Gullickson from Montreal. Gullickson led the staff with a 15–12 record, as 1985's twenty-game ace Tom Browning leveled off at 14–13. With Ron Robinson and lefties John Franco (29 saves) and Rob Murphy, the club had one of the league's better bullpens. Erstwhile ace Mario Soto was 5–10 and underwent arm surgery. At the age of twenty-nine, Soto was for all intents and purposes finished.

For Pete Rose it was an unannounced retirement from active playing. The skipper removed himself from the lineup in late August and did not play again, although there were some vague comments about returning in 1987. In one of his last games, on August 11, Rose set a National League record by rapping out 5 hits in a game for the tenth time. In a way, Rose's feat resembled the dying embers of Babe Ruth's career, when in 1935 the mighty slugger blasted 3 home runs in a game a few days before his worn-out talents forced him into retirement. For Rose, baseball's most prolific collector of base hits (4,256 is the banner number), that 5-hit game in the twilight was the final salvo of his twenty-four-year playing career.

(LEFT) Buddy Bell (1985–1988), the gifted third baseman and son of Gus Bell, gave the Reds some good years toward the end of his career.

(RIGHT) The multitalented Eric Davis (1984–) had 27 homers and 80 stolen bases in 1986.

In 1987, swatting at a ball that seemed suspiciously livelier, both leagues set new home-run records, the National League hammering a new high of 1,824 long ones. Cincinnati's contribution to the cannonading was 192, tied for third highest in the league. For the Reds, Davis was the primary buster with 37, followed by 26 apiece from Parker and Daniels and 22 from Nick Esasky. Davis's 100 RBIs led the club. Daniels, getting into 108 games, batted .334.

Davis began the 1987 season with some sensational blasting, being voted the National League Player of the Month in both April and May, when he hit 19 home runs and drove in 52 runs, accumulating what proved to be half of his season's totals in these departments in the first third of the season (injuries limited him to 129 games).

The Reds led the division from May 29 until early August, when a 4-game tumble in San Francisco began their decline. A 9–20

Outfielder Kal Daniels (1986–1989) swung a .334 bat in 1987.

August buried them 6 games behind the Giants by the beginning of September, which is where they were at season's end.

Injuries to Davis, Daniels, and Esasky, and second baseman Ron Oester hurt, but the sharpest problem in 1987 was the pitching. No starter won more than 10 and the staff logged just 7 complete games, one above the league's record low. This placed a heavy burden on the bullpen, but the Reds had one of the best. Murphy worked in 87 games (a record for major-league left-handers), Frank Williams in 85, and the closer Franco (32 saves) in 68.

Bill Bergesch was dismissed right after the season and replaced by Murray Cook, formerly GM with the Yankees and most recently Montreal. Cook's first important trade attended to the club's pitching needs: on November 6, 1987, he swapped Ted Power and shortstop Kurt Stillwell to Kansas City for

Barry Larkin (1986–   ), latest in the line of fine Cincinnati shortstops.

Bill Gullickson (1986–1987), a 15-game winner in 1986.

Ted Power (1983–1987) about to let fly.

Bullpen stopper John Franco (1984–1989).

shortstop Angel Salazar and left-hander Danny Jackson, only 9–18 in 1987 but a pitcher of acknowledged ability.

With the baseball apparently tranquilized in 1988, 1987's gaudy long-ball statistics declined. Cincinnati's home-run total dropped by 70, to 122, with Davis's 26 leading the team. The club was without a .300 hitter, Barry Larkin's .296 being tops. The gifted young shortstop also stole 40 bases, but made the club uneasy with 29 errors, most by a National League shortstop. The lineup missed Dave Parker, who had been traded to Oakland for pitchers Jose Rijo and Tim Birtsas.

The farm system, which in the past few

Rob Murphy (1985–1988), hard-throwing reliever.

years had been sending outstanding talent to the head of the class, graduated another fine player—the Rookie of the Year, in fact—in third baseman Chris Sabo, who batted .271, hit 40 doubles, and stole 46 bases. Sabo's hustle on the field was evident to the fans, but the rookie also possessed an engaging competitive fervor—an "athletic personality"—that also became evident to the fans, and the new third baseman quickly moved aside the veteran Bell and became a favorite at Riverfront.

Nick Esasky (1983–1988), who played first, third, and outfield.

The league's two top left-handers wore Cincinnati uniforms that year, Jackson dazzling everyone with a 23–8 record and Browning delivering an 18–5 season. Jackson's win total was the highest by a Cincinnati southpaw since Eppa Rixey's 25 in 1922. Browning turned in the most sublime of pitching performances when on September 16, 1988, he pitched a perfect game against the Dodgers, winning by a 1–0 score. Browning had missed an earlier no-hitter, pitching $8\frac{1}{3}$

Eric Davis.

Barry Larkin.

innings of hitless ball in a 12–0 victory over San Diego on June 6 before Tony Gwynn singled in the ninth.

The Reds came within one strike of having two perfect games by their staff. On May 2, Ron Robinson, whose elbow problems were to reduce him to a 3–7 record, had retired the first 26 Montreal batters he faced and had two strikes on pinch-hitter Wallace Johnson when Johnson whacked a single. Robinson then needed relief help to emerge with a 3–2 win.

Jose Rijo, slowed by an aching elbow in August, was 13–8. The bullpen was again strong, with Franco chalking up 39 saves, thanks to the excellent set-up work provided by Murphy and Williams. Added to the staff this year were a trio of young pitchers soon to make an impact at Riverfront: left-hander Norm Charlton, Jack Armstrong, and Rob Dibble, the latter with a fastball that sped toward the plate in the high 90s.

For Dave Concepcion, now forty years old and a utility infielder, it was his nineteenth and final big-league season. No other player has spent as many consecutive years in a Cincinnati uniform.

Playing less than .500 ball until August, the Reds used an 18–9 September to get into second place, where they finished in 1988 for the fourth consecutive time, 7 games behind the Dodgers.

Finishing second is commendable, but four straight years in the slot can become ominous for a manager, and there was some specula-

Chris Sabo (1988–), Cincinnati's Rookie of the Year third baseman in 1988.

tion that Rose's job might be on the line in 1989. For Pete, it had been a frustrating year. A May run-in with umpire Dave Pallone, during which Pete had shoved the umpire, cost the feisty skipper a one-month suspension. But if 1988 was difficult for Rose, 1989 was a nightmare.

Reports began circulating during 1989's spring training session that Rose had in the past wagered on baseball games. If true, this would have placed Pete in violation of professional baseball's rules, which state that anyone employed in the sport who is found guilty of betting on a baseball game runs the risk of a one-year suspension, while a wager involving a game one is involved in carries the penalty of a lifetime ban.

Danny Jackson (1988–1990), who was 23–7 in 1988, left as a free agent after the 1990 season.

Ron Robinson (1984–1990), was one strike away from a perfect game in 1988.

At this point rumors, gossip, and innuendos involving Rose and his known penchant for gambling began to paint large headlines. Rose, admittedly a frequent visitor to horse and dog tracks (which was perfectly acceptable), denied he had ever bet on baseball, and most vehemently denied wagering on games he or his team had participated in.

An investigation into the matter initiated by baseball's recently appointed commissioner Bart Giamatti went on throughout much of the spring and summer. By now there were accusations, denials, testimony, press leaks, court appearances, and injunctions, all of which culminated on August 24, 1989, when the commissioner announced

Marty Brennaman, Cincinnati's long-time announcer.

that Rose had been struck with a lifetime suspension from baseball (subject to appeal for reinstatement after one year). It had been the conclusion of Giamatti and his chief investigator John Dowd that Rose had indeed bet on baseball games, including games played by the Reds, in 1985, 1986, and 1987. While he denied ever having bet on baseball, Rose agreed not to contest the commissioner's ruling. (Soon after the suspension was announced, on September 1, Giamatti suddenly died of a heart attack at the age of fifty-one.) Thus "Charlie Hustle," baseball's most prominent symbol of aggressive play and its all-time leader in hits, was forced from the game that had been his life and livelihood for three decades. (Rose's troubles were to compound. In 1990, after pleading guilty to income tax evasion, he was sentenced to a five-month stretch in a federal prison camp at Marion, Illinois.)

Overshadowed, and no doubt distracted, by the ongoing turmoil of their manager's predicament, the Reds played below expectations in 1989 and finished fifth, 17 games behind the division-winning Giants. Along with Rose's legal problems, the club endured a season of costly injuries. Onto the shelf at one time or another went Danny Jackson (who fell to 6–11), Jose Rijo, and Ron Robinson of the pitching staff; shortstop Barry Larkin (for almost half the season), third baseman Chris Sabo (half the season), second baseman Ron Oester, catcher Bo Diaz, and outfielders Paul O'Neill and Eric Davis.

Catcher Joe Oliver (1989–).

Larkin's injury probably hurt the team the most. Batting .340 when he was selected to the All-Star squad, Larkin injured his elbow making a throw during a skills competition that was part of the All-Star festivities. Except for a few pinch-hitting appearances in September, he was through for the season.

Despite a few weeks on the disabled list, Davis delivered a solid season with 34 homers and 101 runs batted in. Switch-hitting first baseman Todd Benzinger, acquired in a trade that saw Esasky and Murphy go to the Red Sox, supplied some punch with 17 homers.

Browning gave a tattered staff some stability with a 15–12 record, with reliever Rob Dibble the second biggest winner with a 10–5 mark, blinding the league with 141 strikeouts in ninety-nine innings. Franco, who in December was traded to the Mets for Randy Myers in a swap of left-handed relievers, had 32 saves.

Todd Benzinger (1989–).

Tom Browning.

On August 3, 1989, coming off of a 7–19 July, the Reds took out some of their frustrations in a record-making first inning against Houston. En route to an 18–2 shellacking of the Astros, the Reds ran up a major-league record 12 singles while scoring 14 runs.

With Rose's suspension on August 24, coach Tommy Helms was named interim manager for the rest of the season. Then, on November 3, 1989, a new skipper was signed, Lou Piniella.

"Sweet Lou" had been an immensely popular, clutch-hitting outfielder for the New York Yankees from 1974 to 1984. Later, he was sucked into George Steinbrenner's man-

Lou Piniella.

agerial vortex, serving two terms between 1986 and 1988, when he was signed to a vaguely defined "personal services" contract with the Yankees, which he relinquished to accept a two-year contract with Cincinnati.

One of Piniella's first moves was to obtain first baseman–outfielder Hal Morris from the Yankees. To New York went pitcher Tim Leary (whom the Reds had acquired from the Dodgers, along with infielder Mariano Duncan, in a trade involving Kal Daniels).

With Cincinnati's Rose-colored cloud having been lifted, and with a new manager, the Reds tore out of the starting gate in 1990, winning 23 of their first 30, giving the club its best 30-game opening in this century. By June 3 they bossed the division with a hefty 10-game lead. The Giants put on a 16-of-17 charge in June, trimming the lead to 5 games, but by the end of the month the Cincinnati bulge had been rebuilt back to 10.

Hal Morris (1990–), a .340 hitter in 1990.

At the All-Star break the lead was 8 games, but then the Reds slumped, losing 16 of 28 as the Giants came on again, narrowing the gap to 4½ after sweeping the Reds in San Francisco. But once more, under Piniella's intense leadership, the Reds regrouped, and after giving the Giants a battering in a crucial series played a week later in Cincinnati, the lead was back up to 9 games.

The lead proved to be insurmountable, although the Reds gave their followers some uneasy moments in September. With the Dodgers their chief pursuers now, the lead shrank to 3½ games on September 21, but the Reds would not yield another inch, and

Paul O'Neill (1985–) looks like he's right on that pitch.

Eric Davis.

on September 29 clinched the division title. With a record of 91–71, their margin at season's end was 5 games ahead of the Dodgers. In winning their pennant, the Reds achieved a rare distinction—they were the first National League team since the start of divisional play to cover first place every day of the season.

The Reds won despite a so-so year by Davis, who, hobbled by injuries, got into 127 games, hit 24 home runs, and batted .260, although leading the club with 84 RBIs. The team's .265 average led the league, with its top hitter being Morris, who took over first base after Benzinger was injured in late June and never took a step back, batting .340 in 107 games. Duncan, a .235 lifetime hitter,

Rob Dibble (1988–), right-handed member of the "Nasty Boys" bullpen contingent.

Cincinnati's contingent at the 1990 All-Star Game, played at Chicago's Wrigley Field. Back row *(left to right)*: Rob Dibble, Jack Armstrong, Randy Myers. Front row: Chris Sabo *(left)* and Barry Larkin.

Jack Armstrong (1988–), who started the 1990 All-Star Game for the National League.

surprised one and all with a .306 average, while Larkin (acclaimed by many as the league's top shortstop) finished at .301. Billy Hatcher, acquired from Pittsburgh at the start of the season, batted .276, and Sabo, who led the club with 25 home runs, batted .270. O'Neill also batted .270 and contributed 16 homers and 78 RBIs.

The pitching staff was reminiscent of some of those that helped generate Sparky Anderson's Big Red Machine—starters with modest win totals and a superb bullpen. Tom Browning (15–9) was the top winner, followed by Jose Rijo (14–8), who suffered some midseason shoulder problems. Jack Armstrong had started well; he was 10–3 at the All-Star break and had in fact started the All-Star Game for the National League, but arm miseries soon set in and he finished at 12–9.

Randy Myers (1990–), principal stopper of the 1990 Reds.

Norm Charlton (1988–), who started and relieved in the 1990 pennant year.

The bullpen stalwarts, Randy Myers, Rob Dibble, and Norm Charlton (who became a starter when Rijo was sidelined), earned themselves the collective nickname of "Nasty Boys" for their direct and relentless approach to nailing down victories. Myers, the chief closer, had 31 saves and 98 strikeouts in eighty-six innings. Dibble was a blunt instrument on the mound, the instrument being a fastball that singed the air at as much as 100

Chris Sabo.

miles per hour, enabling him to clock 136 strikeouts in ninety-eight innings, an incredible ratio.

Opposing the Reds in the playoffs were Jim Leyland's Pittsburgh Pirates, the somewhat surprise winners of a grueling divisional title fight with the New York Mets. Piniella went with Rijo in the opener at Cincinnati and saw his club squander a 3–0 lead as Pittsburgh came up with a 4–3 win. The Reds evened it in Game 2 as Browning (with the usual Nasty Boy assistance) beat Pirates ace Doug Drabek, 2–1.

In Pittsburgh for Game 3, Piniella started Danny Jackson, just 6–6 for the season but a man with playoff and World Series experience with Kansas City. Jackson pitched well for $5\frac{1}{3}$ innings and then Piniella began running in his full array of Nasties—Dibble, Charlton, and Myers—and the Reds won it, 6–3, thanks to a 2-run homer by Hatcher and a 3-run shot by Duncan. Game 4 saw Rijo (with bullpen help) win, 5–3, with home-run help from O'Neill and Sabo. The Pirates stayed alive with a 3–2 win in Game 5, Drabek beating Browning.

The Reds clinched the pennant with a 2–1 victory in Game 6 at Riverfront, Jackson winning and Myers saving, the decisive run scoring in the seventh inning on a single by pinch hitter Luis Quinones. There was, however, a breathtaking moment in the top of the ninth. With a man on first, the Pirates' Carmelo Martinez shot a drive out to right field that Glenn Braggs (acquired during the sea-

Glenn Braggs (1990–), who made a game-saving catch in the 1990 pennant playoffs against Pittsburgh.

son from Milwaukee), leaping, snared just as the ball was about to flash over the fence for a 2-run homer. A few moments later, the Reds had won their ninth pennant.

For Lou Piniella and general manager Bob Quinn personally, and for the Reds collectively, it was a most satisfying victory, and just ahead lay another victory, one of stunning dimensions.

Cincinnati's World Series opponents were Tony LaRussa's Oakland Athletics, winners of a third straight American League pennant, reigning world champions and as formidable an alignment of talent as baseball had seen in a long time. Galvanized by the star talents of outfielders Rickey Henderson and Jose Canseco, first baseman Mark McGwire, third baseman Carney Lansford; ace pitchers Dave Stewart (a four-time 20-game winner) and Bob Welch (a 27-game winner); and a strong bullpen capped by the nearly unhittable Dennis Eckersley, the Athletics seemed as close to unbeatable as any team of recent years (they had swept the Boston Red Sox in four straight in the American League playoffs).

With the Oakland strength at all stations, talk of a sweep was not considered outlandish. Well, a sweep there was, but the broom was thrust from a completely unexpected direction. In what was perhaps the most extreme of all World Series upsets, Piniella's spirited and superbly performing club took an immediate grip on the A's and never let go.

The Series opened in Cincinnati with a 7–0 Reds victory, Rijo pitching. The Reds were sparked by a first-inning home run by Davis and 3 hits from Hatcher as Dave Stewart, seemingly invincible in postseason play, went down to defeat.

The Reds won a 5–4, ten-inning thriller in Game 2, the winning run scoring on a double by Joe Oliver that came down square on the foul line as the Reds beat another supposedly invincible pitcher, reliever Dennis Eckersley. Hatcher drilled four hits in this one, giving

Billy Hatcher (1990–), the World Series was almost his private stage.

him a Series-record 7 straight hits (he would finish with 9 safe whacks before leaving early in Game 4 with an injury).

With the universe of baseball wondering what was going on here, the Series moved to Oakland, where the Reds moved on with their amazing sweep. On the strength of a 7-run third, Browning and the Nasties made it three straight with an 8–3 win. Sabo was the hitting star, with two home runs and three runs batted in.

Cincinnati won its fifth world championship the following night, as Rijo outpitched

Mariano Duncan *(right)* welcoming home Billy Bates with the winning run in the tenth inning of Game 2 of the 1990 Series. Bates scored on Joe Oliver's double.

A jubilant Cincinnati team celebrating the final out of their stunning sweep of Oakland in the 1990 World Series.

World Series MVP Jose Rijo holding up his trophy. Rijo joined the Reds in 1988 in a trade with Oakland.

Stewart in a tense 2–1 game, the Cincinnati runs scoring in the top of the eighth inning. The winning run, the world championship run, the final run of the 1990 baseball season, was driven in on a sacrifice fly by Morris. Rijo was scintillating, pitching $8^{1}/_{3}$ innings, allowing 2 hits, fanning 9, and retiring the last 20 batters he faced in succession. With one out in the ninth, Piniella brought in Myers and the southpaw member of what was now baseball's most famous bullpen retired the final two batters and a World Series

Marge Schott, Lou Piniella, and general manager Bob Quinn holding up the championship trophy at a post-Series celebration in Fountain Square.

Riverfront Stadium.

victory that can only be described as unexpected, improbable, and unlikely was entered into the books.

With a .317 batting average for the team and a 1.70 ERA by the bullpen, the Reds were not without World Series heroes. Principal among them were Hatcher, whose .750 batting average set a record for a four-game Series; Sabo with 2 home runs and a .563 average; Rijo with 2 victories, and Dibble and Myers, unscored on in a combined eight innings of bullpen work. As soon as the final out had been recorded in Oakland, back home in Cincinnati, Reds fans began filling up Fountain Square, where many a victory had been celebrated, although none as stunning as this.

It was at that point 131 years since George and Harry Wright and their doughty band of colleagues had formed America's first professional baseball team, traveled far and wide, took on all comers and returned home unbeaten. To that galaxy that burns brightly over America, every summer, Cincinnati has contributed its share of stars, from George Wright and Bid McPhee from the century long gone; on through Sam Crawford, Noodles Hahn, Edd Roush, and Eppa Rixey; and on to Ernie Lombardi, Johnny Vander Meer, Bucky Walters and Paul Derringer; to Frank Robinson; and then on to that magical winning machine of Pete Rose, Johnny Bench, Joe Morgan, Tony Perez, and their gifted teammates; to Lou Piniella's astonishing and freshly minted world champions of 1990, who brought home to the cradle of professional baseball a perfect covering: the world championship banner.

APPENDIX

CINCINNATI REDS LEAGUE LEADERS

HOME RUNS

1901	Crawford	16
1905	Odwell	9
1954	Kluszewski	49
1970	Bench	45
1972	Bench	40
1977	Foster	52
1978	Foster	40

TRIPLES

1902	Crawford	23
1905	Seymour	21
1907	Ganzel	16
1909	Mitchell	17
1910	Mitchell	18
1922	Daubert	22
1924	Roush	21
1932	Herman	19
1935	Goodman	18
1936	Goodman	14
1963	Pinson	14
1967	Pinson	13

DOUBLES

1901	Beckley	39
1903	Steinfeldt	32
1905	Seymour	40
1917	Groh	39
1918	Groh	28
1923	Roush	41
1940	McCormick	44
1947	Miller	38
1957	Hoak	39
1959	Pinson	47
1960	Pinson	37
1962	Robinson	51
1974	Rose	45

DOUBLES (*continued*)

1975	Rose	47
1976	Rose	42
1978	Rose	51
1985	Parker	42

HITS

1905	Seymour	219
1916	Chase	184
1917	Groh	182
1938	McCormick	209
1939	McCormick	209
1940	McCormick	191
1955	Kluszewski	192
1961	Pinson	208
1963	Pinson	204
1965	Rose	209
1968	Rose	210
1970	Rose	205
1972	Rose	198
1973	Rose	230
1976	Rose	215

RUNS BATTED IN

1905	Seymour	121
1916	Chase	84
1939	McCorrmick	128
1954	Kluszewski	141
1965	Johnson	130
1970	Bench	148
1972	Bench	125
1974	Bench	129
1976	Foster	121
1977	Foster	149
1978	Foster	120
1985	Parker	125

BATTING

1905	Seymour	.377
1916	Chase	.339
1917	Roush	.341
1919	Roush	.321
1926	Hargrave	.353
1938	Lombardi	.342
1968	Rose	.335
1969	Rose	.348
1973	Rose	.338

WINS

1922	Rixey	25
1923	Luque	27
1926	Donohue	20
1939	Walters	27
1940	Walters	22
1943	Riddle	21
1944	Walters	23
1947	Blackwell	22
1981	Seaver	14
1988	Jackson	23

STRIKEOUTS

1901	Hahn	233
1939	Walters	137
1941	Vander Meer	202
1942	Vander Meer	186
1943	Vander Meer	174
1947	Blackwell	193

EARNED RUN AVERAGE

1923	Luque	1.93
1925	Luque	2.63
1939	Walters	2.29
1940	Walters	2.48
1944	Heusser	2.38

INDEX